Building on Water to
Combat Urban Congestion
and Climate Change

FLOAT!

Koen Olthuis &
David Keuning

FRAM3

Contents

4 ... Introduction

THE FLOATING DUTCHMAN

16 ... Chapter 1

BUILDING FOR CHANGE

44 ... Chapter 2

THE FUTURE ON WATER

72 ... Chapter 3

TECHNOLOGY LEAP

112 ... Chapter 4

HYDROCITY

142 ... Chapter 5

HOLLAND 2.0 DEPOLDERIZED

172 ... Chapter 6

FLOATING LANDSCAPES

204 ... Chapter 7

SUSTAINAQUALITY

232 ... Chapter 8

SEA OF OPPORTUNITIES

262 ... Chapter 9

MOMENTUM

293 ... Index: People, Places & Phenomena

300 ... Footnotes

302 ... Photo credits

304 ... Colophon

THE FLOATING DUTCHMAN

When Koen Olthuis was a young architect, he became fascinated by the structure of the Dutch landscape with its water and land. At that time, living on water was still limited to the well-known traditional houseboats. After two years of combined land and water projects, he started up Waterstudio.NL with Rolf Peters at the end of 2002, the first architecture firm in the world exclusively dedicated to living on water. The company was a pioneer in a new market. To bring the market to maturity, the main focus was to change the perception of the general public. Waterstudio began with an ambitious plan to develop innovative concepts in both technological and urban design fields. The firm conviction that living on water is essentially no different from living on land, just with a different foundation technique, spurred the bureau on to develop types of

4

housing with greater density and higher quality than the usual houseboats in a recreational countryside setting.

In the first few years, it became clear to Olthuis that the market was lagging behind his vision. So Waterstudio started to target the media. Not just in the Netherlands, but worldwide. In a time when new media was rapidly emerging via Internet, and climate change and water issues were receiving a lot of attention because of the flooding in New Orleans, the tsunami in Asia and Al Gore's film *An Inconvenient Truth*, Waterstudio's vision was soon noticed. News teams from Discovery Channel, the *New York Times* and *Newsweek* paid attention to the story. Stimulating questions from journalists resulted in Olthuis starting to think about solutions to the climate problem on an even larger scale. The vision grew rapidly: from water houses to larger complexes, culminating in floating cities and dynamic urban components. At one point, a reporter from BBC Radio described Olthuis in his broadcast as 'the floating Dutchman'. He uses the title now as his nickname.

In 2004, Olthuis came to the conclusion that existing foundations and construction methods were mainly based on the idea that living on water was about individual objects: the starting point was still a house measuring roughly 10 x 10 m. For larger objects, existing boxes were linked together to make a bigger unit. However, it soon became clear that this technique was not good enough for floating urban components, including roads, buildings and green spaces. Olthuis had to find new solutions that were simple, affordable, quick to produce and assemble and, what's more, suitable for many different functions and even multistorey buildings.

The best ideas come out of the blue. Olthuis experienced his eureka moment while he was fretting at night.

The idea was so simple it seemed almost unreal. He wrote it down, and the following morning he was still convinced that it was the answer to the problems in question. The essence of the idea had to do with the way you can lift several books off a bookshelf at the same time: by applying pressure. If you press the sides hard with both hands, the books are squeezed together and the middle ones do not fall down. This is the basic principle for assembling new, extremely large buoyant foundations. Polystyrene and concrete are laid out on the quay like a sandwich and pulled together using draw rails. The platform can then be directly lowered into the water. However, once the platform has been in the water for a long time, the pressure reduces, causing the concrete to fall into the water and the polystyrene foam to float upwards. The trick is to add a layer of concrete to the top of the platform on time. This covering layer forms a single unit with the prefab elements that will now float forever.

An idea does not become reality without the right people and investors. The big breakthrough came when Olthuis met Paul van de Camp, a developer who was looking for a foundation for the hotels he wanted to build on water. Together with his connections and business partners, the idea was born for Dutch Docklands, a developer of large-scale water projects worldwide. The combination of Olthuis's ideas for buoyant foundations and concrete projects granted to Dutch Docklands via Van de Camp's international water lobby generated a stream of innovative concepts.

At the end of 2004, Dutch Docklands received a phone call from a German scout asking for the 'export department'. He was looking for parties to supply floating islands in Dubai. It had to do with a sort of competition where large consortiums were fighting to find favour with Nakheel, the local property developer who controlled almost all the spatial plans. Nakheel wanted to build floating islands in the shape of a poem written by Sjeik Mohammed bin Rashid al Maktoum. The physical size of a company is easily concealed on the Internet, which is why the caller asked for the export department, but Dutch Docklands – the smallest of the competing parties – was a very strong team in collaboration with the Dutch engineering company Royal Haskoning and Waterstudio. Dutch innovation and enterprise resulted in a wonderful plan. The result was that all the other competitors dropped out and Dutch Docklands started on a three-year process of design and innovation. For this reason, it also opened an office in Dubai.

Media attention and inventions such as floating gardens and floating beaches created entirely unique dynamics. The project, which took place in the middle of the boom in Dubai, led to follow-up assignments: a floating mosque, a floating tower and a floating cruise ship terminal: exceptional projects. They were admittedly not implemented, but they were extremely realistic. While only a few years earlier, a floating apartment complex was seen as the maximum achievable, there was now a demand for floating objects that were not just absurdly large, but also provided new answers to genuine requirements and problems.

The designs did not go unnoticed. The combination of ideas for 'depolderization' in the Netherlands as a solution to rising sea levels, together with the conviction that the solutions could be used worldwide in cities located on the water, led to a media climax in 2007 when Olthuis appeared on *Time Magazine's* list of most influential people that year. Magazine readers voted him into position 122, higher than several other architects such as Calatrava, Koolhaas, Nouvel and Hadid. It led to many lectures, publications and visits from television crews from countless different countries. However, progress was slow in Dubai. The realized designs — mostly floating houses — were mainly located in the Netherlands.

The 'New Water' project led to a new breakthrough. Marleen van Giesen, a young project manager from the Dutch Municipalities Bank (BNG) recognized the potential of Waterstudio's ideas and saw the megaconcepts the bureau had thought up for Dubai. She wanted to make use of that expertise to develop and supervise the first real depolderization neighbourhood in the Netherlands, in the west of the country. For that project, the commissioning party had to take a step that is almost unthinkable for Dutch people: from fighting *against* water to living *with* water. In one of the most urbanized regions in the Netherlands, water storage was necessary to prevent flooding caused by heavy rainfall. It forced the municipality, the district water board and the banks to work together. The plan was innovative, because the thinking about the struggle against water led to a solution *behind* the dikes, in the hinterland. Waterstudio was now asked to bring the concepts and ideas that had been the basis for the philosophy all those years into practice. The ambitious plan received visits from abroad even before it was realized. Olthuis stood in the area on many occasions, between the demolished greenhouses on the still-dry bed after it was pumped out, where in the future the water level would rise to chest height. The 'Citadel' project was included in a list compiled by ABC News of the most extreme building designs, due to its status of first floating apartment complex in the world.

The global crisis brought the architectural sector to a virtual standstill and as a result, the already delayed projects in Dubai were ultimately stopped. The floating islands in the shape of a poem were saved for a first production of 10,000 m², but the tender was cancelled at the last moment. But just at that moment, a new market came into the picture; the climate changes pushed the Maldives into the spotlight of world news. The new president, Mohamed Nasheed, issued the message that he was obliged by rising sea levels to buy land in Sri Lanka and relocate his people. A lengthy lobbying procedure via the Dutch embassy, local parties and ultimately the government brought a new climax in 2010, when the government of the Maldives signed a contract with Dutch Docklands. They agreed to develop a floating city, floating islands, floating golf courses, floating hotels and a floating conference centre in a joint venture, as a solution to the problems caused by rising sea levels and also to encourage social and economic advancement.

Building on water has become Koen Olthuis's life's work. It is a passion that is perhaps subconsciously rooted in history. He comes from a family of Art Nouveau architects, engineers and shipbuilders, so he is merging the traditions of his ancestors. His activities take place and find meaningfulness in the perspective of climate change. The coming years will demonstrate whether his vision on 'scarless developments', 'trading places', 'expanding the urban fabric', 'dynamic cities' and 'consumption urbanism' will become fact.

David Keuning

WORKII

NG ON

THE CIT

Y OF TO

MORRO

Oscar Niemeyer stands
proudly in front of a series
of his sketches.

Chapter 1

BUILDING
FOR
CHANGE

Oscar Niemeyer, one of the most famous architects in the world, reached the age of 102 on 15 December 2009, but did not celebrate the occasion at all; he just went to work as usual. 'Turning 102 is crap,' he commented. Niemeyer was born in 1907 in Rio de Janeiro, where he still lives. His fame originates partly from the distinctive, modern buildings he designed in Rio. Many a futuristic building in the capital city of Brasilia was also created by him. He has said more than once that his source of inspiration for these unorthodox buildings, which often have curved forms, is the bodies of Brazilian women. Niemeyer is considered a *bon vivant* and he enjoys his cigars every day. Four years ago, he became a widower, and married his much younger 60 year-old secretary.[1]

Being an architect is the best thing of all; it gives you eternal youth. In a world where star football players are at the end of their careers by the time they reach 35, an architect under the age of 40 is considered to be a 'youngster'. Any architect with a career as long as Niemeyer's experiences a large number of social changes during his lifetime. They exert an influence on the way society builds and on the position of the architect in the hierarchy of the building process. That position is in a constant state of flux, and depends on how capable or incapable the architect is of tackling the problems of his time with creative solutions. In recent years, for example, as a result of worldwide stagnation on the property market, it was largely the developer who called the shots. The role of the architect was marginalized from building principal to façade designer. In the meantime, developers designed standardized and optimized building concepts. As a result, creativity became increasingly unnecessary.

Rising and falling importance of architects.

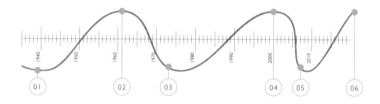

01 1939-1945 World War II	04 2000 Publication of *Superdutch*
02 1961 Publication of *Archigram I*	05 2007-Present Financial Crisis
03 1973-1979 Oil and Energy Crisis	06 Near Future Floating Urbanism

In the 1950s, the role of the architect in the building process also underwent a change. After the Second World War, the conflict of direction between modernism and traditionalism, which had led to heated discussions throughout the whole of Europe before the war, disappeared like snow in summer. The necessity for rapid reconstruction led to a desperate search for increased building output throughout the Western world. The building process was rationalized to the utmost, with the result that the creative freedom of architects was of minor importance for years on end. The monotonous, post-war districts in many European cities are still the unloved reminders of that period.

It is only when substantial changes take place, which create situations in which existing concepts no longer suffice,

that the architect comes into his own again. In the early 1970s, it was resistance to the social monotony of the 1950s and 1960s that increased the creative importance of the architect once again. He was no longer the slave of the developer, but took the initiative and created solutions to the social issues relevant at that time: the rise of individualism and an anti-authoritarian attitude to life. Rem Koolhaas's voice was heard for the first time in 1972, with his 'Exodus, or the Voluntary Prisoners of Architecture'. Later in the decade, Bernard Tschumi made *The Manhattan Transcripts*, which were deeply rooted in the student protests of 1968. In the past, architects and urban designers have always been at the basis of new living environments. People are flexible, they accept change relatively quickly. But imagining the way in which new techniques can lead to new living environments, that is a task for the designers.

The current generation of architects belongs to the 'climate change generation'. In 2010, climate change and urbanization define the social debate and, by extension, the agenda of the designers. One example is the introduction of the LEED certification system, designed to make buildings more environmentally-friendly. Or Brad Pitt's Make It Right Foundation, which overcomes the consequences of hurricane Katrina by commissioning architects to design houses that can survive a flood. Or all the architecture biennials in recent years, in Venice, Rotterdam, Shenzhen and all those other places, which had urbanization as their central theme.

Developed for the Make it Right Foundation, the Float House is a prototype for prefabricated, affordable housing designed by Morphosis. Taking inspiration from the shotgun style houses typical throughout New Orleans, the project was designed to meet the needs of families residing in the Lower Ninth Ward. A flood-safe house that securely floats with rising water levels, the project is adaptable for use in other flood zones throughout the world.

It is up to young architects to think up solutions to the consequences of climate change. In this way, they are working on the cities of tomorrow. Sustainable cities: What do they look like? How do we keep them dry? How do urban structures, and the components from which they are assembled, need to adapt to deal with the stream of new inhabitants? How can the standard of living be maintained or improved? How do we deal with the leftovers of centuries of urban design, with its accompanying urban scars and cultural legacy?

Urbanization and Prosperity

At the moment, for the first time in history, more people worldwide live in towns and cities than in the country. Migration to the city continues unabated. The prediction is that in 2050 70 per cent of the world's population will live in towns and cities. Richard Florida describes how urban structures

grow in his paper *The Rise of the Mega-Region*. Rule 1: they keep on growing; they practically never reduce in size. Rule 2: multiple structures often merge into mega-regions. Where these regions are located and how they develop is illustrated by Florida with satellite images of the earth at night. These images are fascinating; they show the patches of light produced by cities in the dark. If you study the patches more closely, a number of mega-regions stand out, for example New York-Boston-Washington, and Amsterdam-Antwerp-Brussels. There are 40 of these mega-regions in the 200 countries that make up the world. Together, they account for 60 per cent of economic production and 90 per cent of the innovations in the world. According to Florida, these urban regions are by now more important economically than the countries in which they are situated.[2]

City dwellers, with their customs, culture, history and wishes, are reminiscent of a large organism, which needs corresponding urban components and a corresponding urban structure in order to survive. Maintaining that organism's standard of living relies for a large part on the urban infrastructure: the quality and availability of services such as health care, public transport, education, culture, energy and communication. This prosperity varies per country and region.

The greatest challenge for growing metropolises is the maintenance of prosperity levels. The larger the metropolis, the more unmanageable the processes. Prosperity cannot be expressed in absolute numbers alone. Just as important is

The Legatum Prosperity Index is the world's only global assessment of wealth and wellbeing; unlike other studies that rank countries by actual levels of wealth, life satisfaction or development, the Prosperity Index produces rankings based upon the very foundations of prosperity – those factors that help drive economic growth and produce happy citizens over the long term.

■ Indicates strong rank
■ Indicates average rank
■ Indicates weak rank
▨ Insufficient data

CHAPTER 1 | BUILDING FOR CHANGE

the subjective perception of prosperity. The degree of prosperity is therefore dependent on several factors, which are charted by different parties. One of these parties is the British Legatum Institute, which draws up the annual Prosperity Index. Let us examine how Legatum defines prosperity.

Tokyo is one of the most crowded cities in the world.

The Prosperity Index covers 90 per cent of the world population and is based on years of statistical analysis of objective data and subjective reactions to surveys. The data consists of 79 different variables, organized into nine sub-indexes – each identified as fundamental to prosperity in the long term. The performance of individual countries in each sub-index is awarded a score, and the overall Prosperity Index ranking is the result of the averages of the scores achieved by each country in the nine sub-indexes. The countries that perform well in each sub-index achieve the best result in the general ranking.

A few examples of sub-indexes are Economic Fundamentals (a growing, healthy economy that makes the creation of prosperity possible), Education (an accessible, high quality education system that stimulates human development), Health (the physical well-being of the population) and Safety and Security (a safe environment in which people have the opportunity to pursue their personal goals).[3]

Night shot showing the light emission from the world's megaregions.

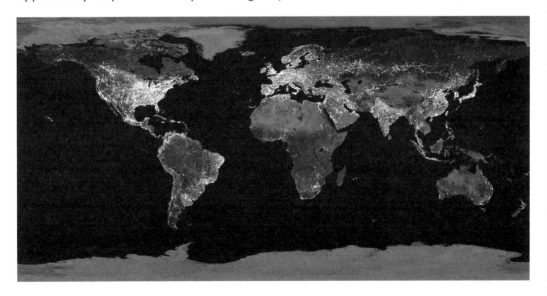

And what turns out to be the case? In all these sub-indexes, the urban environment plays a significant role. In order to be able to pursue all the set goals, roads and buildings are of course necessary. The state of the physical living environment is therefore an important factor when defining the level of prosperity.

In growing cities, this infrastructure almost always comes under pressure. On the one hand, a high number of inhabitants is important for the quality of services. After all, the greater the demand, the more that can be invested in the services. But, on the other hand, expanding metropolises are increasingly difficult to maintain. That means that maintaining the infrastructure will become an important challenge in the near future.

New Density

In order to retain and improve the infrastructure, and in so doing, safeguard prosperity with all its accompanying services, a minimum number of consumers is required (preferably more than eight million, according to the American sociologist and urbanist Saskia Sassen[4]), who additionally live in a relatively compact city. If the surface area becomes too large, the cost-effectiveness of the logistics is no longer optimal. The task Florida assigns to growing metropolitan regions is: 'How to achieve greater density?'

Urban density is usually expressed in population per square kilometre or square mile. The possibilities for increasing urban density are limited. Density has increased dramatically in the last 200 years, but by now the beaten tracks have pretty much come to a dead end. The amount of built-up square metres and the number of inhabitants per square kilometre have increased mainly as a result of the development of high-rise buildings (into the air) and the metro (into the ground). Building even higher would result in an extremely vertical city, or even more functions could be located underground. Stacking certainly does increase density, but not necessarily the quality of life. Furthermore, it is principally an option for the centres of metropolises, due to the high investments required for these extreme building types.

Urbanization also results in an increase in the paved surface area. An increased level of paving of the landscape (percentage of paved area per square kilometre or square

mile) has a significant influence on the sewerage and drainage capacities required in an urban area. More paving leads to more problems with rainfall. Large cities worldwide are faced with the challenge of adapting their water management. Water storage and, in more general terms, space for water, are necessary elements here.

As much as 90 per cent of the 100 largest cities in the world are located on water. Furthermore, these cities have a substantial amount of water in the city itself, in the form of lakes, rivers, canals, harbours, bays or the open sea. In the largest cities, a considerable percentage of the ground area is therefore open water.

So the answer to the question 'How to grow more dense?' is obvious: make use of the open water landscape in the cities for building development. That is New Density: building more per square kilometre of city is only possible by making use of the water.

On 22 December 2008, a heavy rain caused the streets to flood in São Paulo, Brazil, disrupting the normal flow of vehicular traffic.

Impulses for Change

Urban structure is built up from components, such as buildings, parks and infrastructure. City dwellers with their wishes and demands try to function the best they can as a living organism within these components. However, this is no more than an attempt, because the

demands and wishes are more dynamic than the urban accommodation. Buildings are static: once they have been built, they
have to last for a considerable number of years. Buildings can
hardly keep up with the social, political, technical and economic impulses of the city. Their lifespan is too long for that.
In order to understand which changing demands have to be
met by buildings during their lifespan, it is important to know
which developments can lead to a change in spatial demand.

Social Change

Old film and television images are reliable witnesses of social
systems from the past. Images from just 50 years ago show a
world that is now completely alien to people. The composition of families and the size of households in the West changed
significantly after the war. Personal life also changed radically in
the 1950s and 1960s. Families became smaller and the number
of households increased.

Working on a Saturday was completely normal after
the war; these days, part-time work is quite common, or
that both parents work. The number of annual holidays has

increased; at the same time, the time needed to carry out household tasks has been reduced by mechanization. Washing machines, cookers, vacuum cleaners, off-the-peg clothing and refrigerators do the work now. Children leave home later; old people just keep getting older. The average life expectancy has risen in the last half-century from roughly 70 to 82 years. Ageing of the baby boom generation is now in full swing. That has resulted in an increased demand for apartments for the elderly, multiple-generation homes, sheltered accommodation and flexible, adaptable homes. It is no longer a matter of course for people to live and work in the same city. And in people's spare time, social networks do not stop at the city limits. The demand for mobility is greater than ever before. These social changes have consequences for the demands people make on their residential surroundings and their homes.

Shortly after the Second World War, the hierarchy of the class system, which divided people into working class, middle class and upper class, was very much alive in a large part of Western Europe. Daily life in the Netherlands, for example, took place in one of the four sociopolitical groups: Protestant,

Roman Catholic, Social Democratic or Liberal. Which school you went to, who your employer was, what you did in your spare time; it all depended on your background. It was practically impossible and not at all usual to switch groups. On the contrary; it was normal to accept the situation and conform to your inherited role. Towns and cities are completely different now. There is no question of sociopolitical groups anymore; the only criterion now that determines where you live or where you can move to is money. Services are mainly centralized, which has led to the increased importance of the car as a means of transport. The effects of the removal of traditional religious and sociopolitical barriers have also had repercussions on the demands made on the urban environment. The social composition of the city is not as clear as it used to be.

MORE PAVING LEADS TO MORE PROBLEMS WITH RAINFALL

Political Change

Anarchism, Communism, Conservatism, Corporatism, Ecologism, Falangism, Fascism, Islamism, Leninism, Liberalism, Maoism, Marxism, Nationalism, Pragmatism, Socialism and Stalinism: a short enumeration of several well-known and lesser-known political movements. Each has its own division of power and corresponding symbols of power in the form of architecture. Political systems have considerable repercussions on the building programme and its appearance. These days, political systems are reasonably stable, but often that does not last for more than a few decades.

Democratic systems act as a buffer between the urge for change shown by the city councillors and the interests of the city dwellers. In democracies such as in Western Europe, the term of government is four years. That has an inhibitive effect on the development of the city. After all, every plan produced must show results in the short-term, in order to safeguard the next term of government. Large-scale urban alterations require decades, however.

It is sometimes a good thing that governmental thirst for action is curbed. Every year, millions of tourists visit Amsterdam. One of the highlights is the network of city canals. They were once part of the logistic system and the water management of the city. It is almost impossible to imagine now, but in the 1960s, a few politicians made an attempt to have the canals filled in. Shortage of space and a lack of cultural insight led them to submit plans that would have meant a metamorphosis for the city.

In contrast, everyone who drives through Paris now can enjoy the beautiful promenades, the straight boulevards and clear structure, often without realizing that these are all the consequence of enormous interventions in the historical city. Practically all of them are the work of Georges Eugène Baron Hausmann, during the reign of Emperor Napoleon III. The aim of the interventions was not so much the beautification of the city; they were intended to ensure that opposition and riots could be controlled. The boulevards are sight lines between military positions, which facilitated the overview and

View from the Arc de Triomphe of two tree-lined promenades, Avenue Hoche and Avenue de Friedland, in Paris. In the distance Avenue Hoche merges with the Parc de Monceau, an English style garden, which houses a collection of scaled architecture figures including a traditional Dutch windmill.

communication over long distances within the city. Paris was formerly a maze of narrow streets and communes, where control was almost non-existent. Politics formed the impulse for urban development.

When a political system falls, the physical changes in a city are often drastic, too, because political ideology can be so clearly presented by architecture in particular. Berlin is perhaps the best place to see what sort of influence politics can have on a city. After the split, at the end of the Second World War, the German capital was able to develop for 40 years in accordance with two different political lines: communism as opposed to capitalism. Now, 20 years after the reunification, the traces have not yet been eradicated, by any means. The *Plattenbau* (industrialized building system of prefabricated concrete slabs pieced together without a framework) and the Stalinist boulevards in former East Berlin still form an uneasy union with the more traditional Western block organization. The lifespan of the buildings here is considerably longer than the length of time the political system was in place, but the buildings do partly define the soul of the city.

The world is full of buildings that illustrate political aims. For example, the imposing buildings designed by Albert Speer that played an important role in Nazi propaganda. Or the iconic architecture in the UAE, with the Burj Khalifa in Dubai as highest tower in the world. And the American suburbs as the ultimate habitat for the middle class in the capitalist politics of the USA. Politics give huge impulses to urban structures and their components.

Technological Change

New techniques also provide opportunities to organize cities differently. The invention of steel construction, prefabricated elements, the lift, the underground, sewage systems, asphalted roads, central heating, double glazing: whatever you can think up in terms of technological progress, it has changed the face of the city and had a deep influence on urban life. Cities and technological progress are inextricably linked. Structural or engineering innovation is traditionally the ultimate means to show off power. The competition for the largest dome, the longest bridge or the highest tower: that form of competition is as old as the city itself. Today, too, technological progress is essential for the way in which cities function and present

themselves to the outside world. Blobs, a bridge at a height of 300 m in the CCTV tower in Beijing, megalomaniac buildings initiated by French presidents: technological feats are an excellent marketing tool and the city is used as the parade ground on which to display these achievements.

Technological progress is not static. Thanks to information technology and globalization, new techniques spread more quickly than in the past. In addition, they become common property increasingly quickly. New technology, both in the field of construction and outside, will change the face of cities even further in the future. There is no escape from that.

Economic Change

The availability of money and the level of growth or contraction in prosperity fundamentally influence the way in which cities plan their space. Economies are not static. Developing

countries can make huge leaps forward, whereby the demand for urban structure totally changes. A typical sight in Beijing is, for instance, the so-called *hutongs*: residential neighbourhoods that have existed for 700 years and whose origins date back to the period after the invasion of Genghis Khan. These traditional, walled districts with alleyways sometimes only 40 cm wide and streets narrower than 9 m, often lack the most

elementary sanitation. Electricity is often not available, either. Now that China is flourishing economically, the *hutongs* are quickly disappearing as a result. In 1950, there were around 6000 in Beijing; now, in 2010, there are less than 3000.

In times of economic prosperity, nearly every client wants an extreme building. In current times, too, economic impulses can quickly have an effect. Take Dubai, for instance. That is an overwhelming city, which has sprouted unbelievably quickly. Just 30 years ago, nomads with camels walked over unpaved roads on this spot. Now the highest building in the world is located here. Dubai began with a unique collection of impulses: enough space, enough money, huge ambitions and a simple political constellation run by a limited number of people, led by the Emir Sheikh Mohammed bin Rashid Al Maktoum. That gave the city an incredible impetus. Not everyone is equally enthusiastic about Dubai, but the city shows how fast vision, money and power can influence urban structure.

New Flexibility

Changes in the spatial demands and wishes of city dwellers never happen in isolation, but in a continuous interaction with other demands and wishes. In addition, different impulses struggle for domination. Now, in 2010, it is climate change and urbanization that exert the greatest pressure on the infrastructure and the urban landscape.

In the last 100 years, cities have not only had to deal with more changes than average in the centuries before, but the speed at which the changes take place and their magnitude (due to increased population numbers and increased technological possibilities) make it virtually impossible to anticipate the changes beforehand. The high building density in contemporary metropolises leads to spatial interventions having a greater impact than was previously the case. The high complexity of the modern city requires a high level of flexibility, so that changing spatial requirements can find a place within the existing structures.

The speed at which changes spread out has also continued to grow in the past decades. Technological progress keeps speeding up due to computerization and globalization. Internet naturally has a big effect on the spreading of innovations. Social networks and news platforms such as Twitter and Facebook did not yet exist five years ago and have a significant impact on the way in which people communicate. The role played by Twitter in the spread of information in political regimes such as Iran is considerable, because everyone can spread news without censorship. The student protest on 4 June 1989 in Tiananmen Square in Beijing, during which hundreds of people lost their lives, would undoubtedly have ended differently if Twitter had existed then. In this way, social networks have an indirect influence on the physical appearance of the large city. After all, history has shown time and time again that a change of regime is accompanied by radical spatial interventions in the city.

By now, it must be clear: there is an area of tension between the long lifespan of the urban environment and the quickly fluctuating demands and wishes of the city dwellers.

THE ULTIMATE FORM OF FLEXIBILITY IS FLOATING BUILDINGS

The extent to which the urban environment is capable of meeting the changing requirements within these components and structures determines the flexibility of the city. The design of urban components and expansions that can hold their own for a longer time, without knowing all the things that are going to change, is called planning for change. Planning for change is only possible if metropolises are flexible.

Flexibility can be realized by actions that include fitting in a considerable amount of open space, or space that is filled with a low economic value. Those are mainly functions with a short period of usage, so that the ground they take up can easily be released for unexpected spatial requirements.

A 25-storey floating hotel tower, in Dubai, UAE, rotates one degree every minute, providing the guests with a constantly changing perspective of the city. Designed by Waterstudio in collaboration with Dutch engineering company DHV and offshore industry specialist Vuyk, the 100-m. steel and glass building resides on a floating foundation that measures only 11 m in depth. A fixed floating boulevard connects the tower to the city's shore.

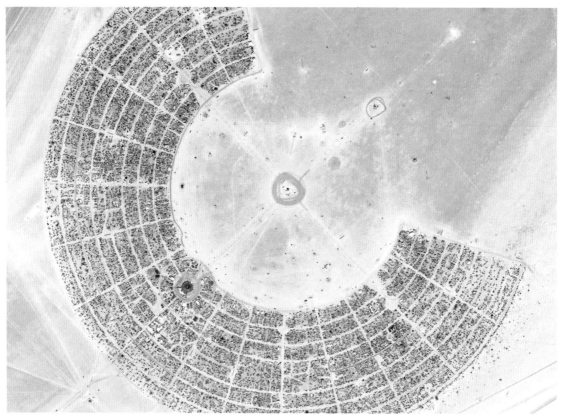

Aerial view of the flexible city, which has become a staple of the Burning Man festival.

One example of this is the student apartments in the Dutch cities of Delft and Amsterdam. A few years ago, there was a huge demand in a short space of time for student accommodation. They are now housed in reusable cargo containers that can easily be relocated. Planning permission for the placing of the containers is easy to obtain, due to the temporary nature of the function.

Camper vans are even easier to move. Every year, the Burning Man festival is held in the Nevada desert in the USA. In the space of a few days, a city made up of thousands of camper vans is created, complete with roads and other facilities. Days filled with culture, art, parties and personal expression are brought to a close with the burning of the wooden man on the temporary main square, in the middle of the settlement. Afterwards, the city is dismantled again. Without any traces remaining, the desert is once again returned to an empty space. It is almost impossible to be more flexible.

A contrasting form of flexibility is, paradoxically, solidity. Buildings with a surplus of space and a solid structure provide opportunities for accommodating different functions

in the course of time. Churches which become empty
due to lessening religious interest and former industrial
buildings in old town centres can be rebuilt as homes or
take on new functions.

The ultimate form of flexibility is floating buildings.
By uncoupling the permanent connection between building
and location, the building becomes a product that can be used
during its lifetime by different owners at different locations.
The possibility of relocation means that a site can be used
for different purposes in the course of time.

Floating buildings have a considerable number of
advantages. They make it possible to bring extremely large
and space-intensive events to the city, without having to
reserve space for them years in advance. The Olympic Games,
for instance, usually provide the city with a positive impulse,
at least in theory. They bring economic advantages and
provide an opportunity for initiating urban renewal projects.
The Olympic Park in Barcelona, for example, restored the
relationship with the waterfront. The current city dwellers
are still reaping the benefits, almost 20 years on.

But there is also one big disadvantage: afterwards,
the city is left with overcapacity in sports facilities. For
example, people visiting Beijing now can see that the
impressive stadium designed by Herzog & De Meuron and
the beautiful swimming hall designed by the Australian architect duo PTW have fallen into disuse. If those buildings had
been implemented as floating structures, they could have
been moved to locations with a real requirement.

The same is true of London, where the Olympic
Games will take place in 2012. The design bureau EDAW
drew up the London 2012 Olympic Park Master Plan. The
first designs date from 2003 and have been adapted a few
times since then. Economic considerations were of over-
riding importance for these adjustments. For instance, the
Olympic Park was reduced in size because it turned out to be
too expensive to clear a valuable piece of land in the middle
of the capital city years in advance, and then keep it clear.

If the Olympic Delivery Authority had chosen to additionally make use of the water of the Thames, immediately adjacent to the park, then, taking the same useable surface area,
not only the amount of space taken up and the level of invest-
ment would have been lower, but also the time taken up would

have been less: it would not have been necessary to free up the land ten years in advance. Instead, floating stadiums and other facilities could have been moored a mere two years in advance. They could have been built in dry docks, far away from the centre, so that the city dwellers would have been spared the nuisance caused by such large-scale building projects. And, directly after the Games, they could have been moved to locations with a requirement for such facilities.

But it is never too late for good resolutions. In 2016, the Olympic Games will take place in Rio de Janeiro, Oscar Niemeyer's city. There is plenty of water there, and because of the city's situation up against mountain slopes, there are very few building locations available. Rio de Janeiro would be able to make world history as the location for the first

IT IS UP TO THE CLIMATE CHANGE GENERATION NOW

floating Olympic Games. A strange idea? Not for people who dare to think outside the box. It is up to the climate change generation now.

TOWAR

RDS FLOA

ATING FC

OUNDA

IONS

Floating houses in Amsterdam IJburg, designed by Marlies Rohmer.

Chapter 2

THE
FUTURE
ON WATER

In 2010, a television crew from Discovery Channel's *Next World* came to the Netherlands for an interview. To give the viewer an idea of what it's like to live on the water, they visited a number of water houses that had just been completed in IJburg, designed by Waterstudio. The journalist was enthusiastic and asked the architects: 'I expect you would also love to have your own house on IJburg, right?' The answer was: 'Absolutely not!' The houses are certainly attractive, but living on a landing stage with no garden or garage is not really ideal. We wouldn't fancy struggling over a metal jetty in all weathers with our bags of shopping which subsequently make the house lean over when we set them down in a corner of the kitchen.

Two single-family floating housing units, designed by Waterstudio, located in the developing IJburg district.

The interviewer looked very surprised by this revelation and asked why they hadn't been designed differently. The explanation is simple: the regulations for building on water in IJburg were drawn up ten years ago, using the now-superseded perceptions prevalent at that time, and without sufficient knowledge of stability or market demand. The interviewer wanted to show the cream of the crop in terms of floating housing in the Netherlands, but had only managed to find an example of 'old school' living on the water.

However, the tale of the 'boathouses' on IJburg certainly makes an interesting case study. IJburg is a new residential development rising up from a series of artificially filled-in islands, located to the east of Amsterdam. The floating houses in the water neighbourhood are three storeys high. They have precisely fixed maximum measurements (a floor plan of 7 x 10 m) and a precisely fixed maximum draught (1.5 m). Civil servants specified these dimensions, but they lead to completely instable boats. Anyone could have worked that out. If you think about it, mass situated low in a floating building is no problem. In that situation,

it works like a buoy. If mass is situated high and the height exceeds the width, as in IJburg, the construction becomes instable. As a result, 11 of the 12 houses listed to begin with. A solution had to be found using extra buoyancy, which was extremely expensive to install. It meant an unforeseen expense of tens of thousands of euros per boat, charged to the owners.

However, it was easy to understand why the regulations were drawn up as they were. The pen pushers looked at the existing boathouses already present in the city, and failed to realize that the houses on IJburg would have three storeys instead of one, that 7 x 10 m is in fact a very instable size, and that the boathouses on IJburg, unlike the traditional boathouses in the city centre, would have to conform to the Building Regulations. That means a much heavier method of building, with the paradoxical consequence that they are much less stable than traditional water homes that do not have to conform to all sorts of regulations. This example makes it clear that, in order to take full advantage of the possibilities for building on water, looking to the future is more advisable than looking to the past.

On Steigereiland in the IJmeer, Amsterdam, Marlies Rohmer has created adaptable floating housing blocks based on the reconfiguring of basic modular units and the insertion of selectable kit-of-parts components.

Floating house in De Hoef, the Netherlands, designed by Waterstudio. The houseboat is embedded into a traditional waterside plot. From the front yard it has no visible connection to the water, the back patio tells a different story.

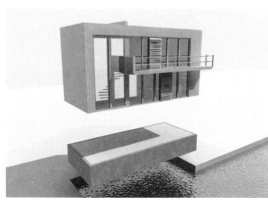

Exploded axonometric drawing showing the logic of the house's floating foundation. The house has two floors and it is founded on a concrete hull, 1.2 m deep and as large as the house itself.

Closing the Gap

Living on water will not become 'mainstream' overnight; it's still a niche market. To emerge from that niche, it will have to discard its characteristics. In the past, a water house in the Netherlands was a type of housing reserved for free spirits, pioneers and DIY enthusiasts, but certainly not something the majority of the population would choose to live in. In order to change that, the external appearance and availability of water houses, in particular, must change. Furthermore, until recently, a building with floating foundations in the Netherlands was not considered the equal of one planted firmly in the ground.

'Closing the gap' means that floating houses need to become the equal of traditional houses on land, in every respect: in comfort, quality and price. Comfort means that the stability and building physics must meet the same requirements imposed on houses on land by the Building Regulations. With the help of the right technology, listing and noticeable increases in building movement can be minimized to such an extent that they can measure up to the relevant requirements placed on, for instance, high-rise buildings. In addition, the exterior space and accessibility contribute to comfort. The provision of parking spaces and gardens on the water will also need to grow.

If you buy a house on water, you need to be able to assume that the materials and maintenance are equivalent to a house built on land. A water house should have the same lifespan as a land house. The only essential difference between a house on water and a house on land is related to the foundations, not the structure.

At the moment, building on water is still relatively expensive, because it only happens on a small scale. Furthermore, in almost every case the house is not built on location, but in one of the water house factories spread throughout the Netherlands and situated on the water. By switching to building water houses in large numbers in dry docks and subsequently 'launching' the houses, there is no reason at all for running up higher building costs than an equivalent house on land with, for instance, a concrete basement. In terms of costs, floating foundations are similar to a basement; however, savings can be made on the pile foundation.

How Strange are Floating Foundations in the Netherlands?

In the Netherlands, there are two main types of foundations in use. The higher-positioned, dry regions of the Netherlands consist principally of sandy ground. In those areas, spread foundation is used when building. That is a method of foundation where the walls have a broadened foot that rests on the bearing substratum.

For the low-lying regions of the Netherlands that are wet and boggy, pile foundation is applied. The capital city, for example, is completely founded on piles. Traditionally, wooden foundation piles were used. Amsterdam is built on marshy ground. If the ground is not consolidated before you start construction, the buildings subside. The Royal Palace on

WATER IS 'THE NEXT BIG THING'

the Dam in Amsterdam, for example, was founded in 1665 on 13,659 wooden piles. In Amsterdam, there is a bigger forest under the ground than above ground! These days, mainly concrete foundation piles are used.

Spread foundation is often cheaper than pile foundation, but it does require a good ground base. In areas of clay and peat, it is often not possible to realize a spread foundation because settlement would be too great. However, spread foundation is certainly possible in areas with an underlayer of sand.

Fluctuating groundwater levels in Dutch water cities such as Haarlem, Gouda and Amsterdam harm the wooden pile foundations underneath the old buildings. Pile rot is a slumbering threat that will cause serious problems in the old city centres in the decades to come, all the more because rainfall can become more severe due to climate change. The capacity of the pumping stations is not designed for these extremes everywhere, which means that water levels in cities can be expected to fluctuate more and more.[5]

Many buildings with basements in the wet regions of the Netherlands have friction pile foundations. This means that the building does not rest on the piles, just the opposite in fact. The friction between the piles and the base layer keeps the building down; it would otherwise start to rise due to the upwards pressure of the groundwater! The basements lie partly in the groundwater in these cases.

Floating foundations work more or less on the same principle. Buoyant objects experience an even upward force from the water they displace, as Archimedes had already discovered 2.5 centuries BCE. In the Netherlands, there are currently 16,000 water houses, but at least half of them are located more or less in the mud. Mud is actually just thick water. The difference between a house with a basement in a marshy area or a water house in the mud is, technically speaking, extremely small. The disadvantage of floating foundations is that the stability of small houses is a point of attention. One advantage is that the house goes up and down in unison with a fluctuating water level. In a wet country such as the Netherlands, a floating foundation is an entirely logical method of foundation.

A Scenario for the Next 100 Years

A hundred years is a long time. Try to imagine what city life looked like a century ago, for example. There were no cars, no aviation, no e-mail and no massive suburbs. European cities consisted of an old centre, often dating largely from the Middle Ages, with a few extremely modest expansions outside the former city walls. The people who could afford it moved around by carriage. The post was also sent in the same way, so it took days or weeks to reach its destination. In between the cities, there was virgin countryside, with an almost exclusively agricultural function. Anyone who could have predicted what the cities would look like in 100 years time would have been considered crazy. And yet, everything that is now reality was unimaginable a century ago.

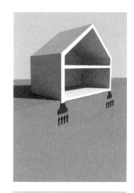

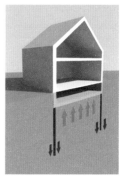

Spread (slab on grade), wooden-pile, friction-pile and floating foundation diagrams.

Designed for mooring three of world's largest cruise ships, the cruise terminal, by Waterstudio, is a massive 700 x 700 x 700 m floating vessel. Located off the coast of Dubai the terminal is only slightly smaller in scale than the Burj Khalifa skyscraper laying down. Structurally, it's three large steel ships, clad in aluminum, coupled together at the ends. At a specific point one of the three ends of the triangular shape rises out of the water 76 m, providing access to an inner harbor for smaller ships and boat taxis. That part is built similar to a building crane, a steel space structure. Designed for real estate development company Nakheel, the proposed terminal has 90,000 m² of usable space distributed over one continuous floor. This unique lightweight structure manages to only have a draught of 2 m, present-day cruise ships generally have a draught of 8 to 10 m, with the water on the mooring site having a depth of 12 to 15 m.

Today, it is just as impossible to imagine what urban life will look like 100 years from now, particularly because developments in society are taking place faster and faster. In 2000, for example, there were hardly any examples of floating projects bigger than a house. These days, large buoyant complexes and floating high-rise buildings can be found in the renderings of many an architectural firm. JDS drew the all-inclusive Wellness Island Mermaid 2.0, Arup Biomimetics designed the Ocean City Syph for the Australian population that migrated from land to sea because of the sky-rocketing value of disappearing land. Waterstudio designed a floating harbour for cruise ships, buoyant high-rise buildings and floating islands for Dubai.

Where planning professionals come up against the physical boundaries of land – because of urbanization, lack of space and rising sea levels – the freedom of floating developments on water begins. Water is 'the next big thing', also in the area of urban expansion possibilities. It is present in practically every metropolis and is generally not used, at least to best advantage. Technical innovations, such as floating buildings, plots and islands, open up an enormous potential for new urban development locations, in one fell swoop.

Spatial pressure and the ever-rising price of land in metropolises ensure that, bit by bit, this sort of innovation will become cost-effective. The economic potential is by now so high that it is worthwhile to take the existing maritime technologies developed in the shipping, oil platform and off-shore industries and apply them to floating constructions, where people can live, work and enjoy their leisure.

The Twenty-First Century on Water in Four Steps

Cities were, almost without exception, founded close to water. Water is a primary necessity of life and the basis for trade. It is logical for cities to grow away from the water, round the old centre, due to lack of space. The highest price per square metre generally remains in the old centre. And, in addition, the highest square metre price of all is usually on the water. Cities could benefit from expansion onto the water. Singapore, Monaco, Hong Kong, New York's Manhattan, Seoul or Bombay: they are all short of space but have more than enough water.

Trading places in three steps. A park is relocated on the water to allow for urbanization of its former location.

How will these metropolises develop on the water? As descibed before, urban structures need to become denser and more flexible to preserve the same level of prosperity. Building on water is the solution to shortage of space: water provides space without having a negative effect on existing functions. But what are the stages involved? In a future scenario for the coming century, four steps are distinguishable, based on economic assumptions.

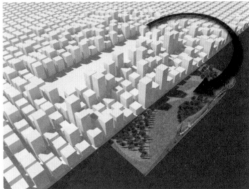

2010-2020: TRADING PLACES

The first step in our vision of the future is trading places. Trading places is relocating functions that take up a lot of space but have a low economic value onto the water. That makes it possible to rebuild highly profitable functions in high density on the land freed up in this way.

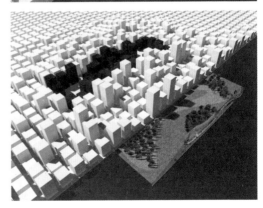

Mermaid 2.0 is a speculative wellness island designed by JDS. The floating island is a mixed-used destination composed of gardens, luxury hotel, housing block, a shopping district and various wellness-based facilities.

Examples of functions that take up a lot of room but have a low economic value are sports grounds, green areas, commercial greenhouses, golf courses and boulevards. These types of functions are very often situated on locations where the pressure of urbanization threatens their continued existence. These are prime candidates for relocation onto the water. Their low load and large surface area provide a great deal of stability, which makes them eminently suitable for placement on simple floating foundations.

Trading Places in the Agricultural Sector

Recently, two trends have become apparent in the agricultural sector. The first is the increasing pressure of urban developments on the space available for agriculture. Farming land is being squeezed out. The second trend is the rising demand for self-sufficiency in metropolises, which has led to city farming in various places.[6] At the moment, agricultural products fly round the whole world before they land on your plate.[7] The desire to make every product available to the consumer, regardless of the season, leads to dragging products all over

The City Farm in Chicago, a sustainable vegetable farm located near the Cabrini-Green and the Gold Coast neighbourhoods of the city, provides produce to some of the city's finest restaurants.

the place on an unbelievably large scale. Meat from Argentina, for instance, is processed in China and ends up in the freezer of a chain of shops in Europe. Dependency on this sort on vulnerable logistics is reduced if cities cultivate their own products. That is the ideal situation. However, in practice, there is hardly any room for this type of self-sufficiency. Floating agriculture in and on urban water can provide a solution for both trends.

While the spatial pressure on the agricultural sector increases, there is a trend that started in the sector itself towards larger and more efficient commercial greenhouses, as a result of growing competition in this field. By building floating greenhouses, bigger and more efficient greenhouse complexes can be realized, while on land, on the location that is freed up, houses can be built. In the Netherlands, which largely consists of water, this is an economically viable option. There's a prototype for a floating greenhouse in Naaldwijk. This project, which was completed on 7 December 2005 by Dura Vermeer, is partly meant as a solution to the spatial demands involved in greenhouse cultivation. It is still there, in all its glory, and is used as an exhibition and information centre these days.

Trading Places in the City Centre

Social changes are a continuous process. How people fill their time with education, religious faith and leisure activities can change significantly in just one or two decades. That has consequences for the spatial organization of the city. School locations are merged of perhaps decentralized. Leisure time is spent less and less at home, and more and more in lifestyle centres specially designed for the purpose, with a shopping centre, cinema, fitness clubs and other facilities. The rise of Islam, Buddhism, *Ietsism* (a Dutch word that translates as 'Somethingism' and means an unspecified belief in some higher force) and, in particular, the individualization of religious faith, these days experienced behind the computer

Floating Pentecostal church designed by Waterstudio.

instead of in church, have all led to a reduction in demand for traditional church buildings in Europe. These types of changes can be easily accommodated in flexible buildings on the water, while on land the discarded buildings and locations can be redeveloped.

In Amsterdam, for example, an innovative developer came to Waterstudio with the idea of relocating a growing religious community, the Pentecostal church, who were located in a building on expensive ground in the capital, to a floating church building in the Slotermeer district. The developer had calculated that new-build on the church's old location would yield enough money to realize the new floating church building and still make a profit. Unfortunately, the plan never came to fruition, because a mooring permit failed to materialize, but the economic model was certainly interesting.

Trading Places between Socioeconomic Classes

Another form of trading places is the shift in the groups of people who find the water an interesting place to settle. As already mentioned, the Netherlands has 16,000 residential water objects. In the Netherlands, living on water was, until a few years ago, an inferior type of housing and did not exactly attract the top segment of the property market. In the last five years, however, there has been a significant change here. Old boathouses on attractive water locations are being bought up for their mooring places, after which expensive high-quality water houses are built to take their place. The rich have rediscovered the water. This shift is the motor behind the market for boathouse builders in the Netherlands.

For Waterstudio, the change in target group for water locations was the driving force to start the company. With the arrival of clients with a substantial budget, the possibilities and the quality of floating buildings could take giant steps forwards. In order to make new forms of living possible, the existing regulations, which were drawn up for traditional boathouses, had to be reinterpreted. A creative solution that still meets all the requirements is an enormous challenge.

In Aalsmeer, for example, Waterstudio built a water house in 2004, using the mooring permit of an old boathouse. The house could only measure 25 x 6 m. For the client, that was not big enough. By studying the regulations, it transpired that nothing had been prescribed about the amount of space allowed under the water line. As a result, it was possible to build an entire storey under water. The quality of the finishing is extremely high. An integrated lift transports a large wardrobe from the upper storey to the lower, where seasonal clothing can be interchanged in the walk-in closet. A cinema under water gives the house its finishing touch.

Waterhouse in Aalsmeer, designed by Waterstudio, with underwater cinema and electrically revolving warderobe.

CHAPTER 2 | THE FUTURE ON WATER

Trading Places between the City and Environs

Urbanization leads to an increase in density in the cities. Public facilities and green areas such as parks shrink in size. That also reduces the quality of life in the city. Relocation of these types of facilities to the water, where they can also be extended if necessary, provides cities with the added value they need so badly in the competitive international arena.

In 2009, for example, Dutch Docklands received a request from Seoul to carry out a feasibility study into a golf course on water. Seoul is surrounded by mountains and is situated on the Han: an enormous river 1 km wide and, within the city limits, 41 km long. The mountains and the river have always been seen as obstacles, so that the city has hardly any

MOST METROPOLISES ARE SHORT OF SPACE BUT HAVE MORE THAN ENOUGH WATER

room for expansion. However, if you see the river as building land, suddenly you have 41 km^2 of the most level, horizontal building land you could wish for, right in the centre. That offers plenty of opportunities for new development.

Golf is one of the most popular sports in South Korea. But golf courses take up a lot of space, and that space is just not available. Golf fans can only enjoy their sport far outside the city. In the city, there is only room for driving ranges, enclosed by large tent nets. By implementing golf courses as floating constructions, they can be relocated to the centre of the city. There is an additional advantage: visually and recreationally, they are an enormous improvement on the hard concrete quays that characterize the Han River at the moment.

Now that building on water no longer has technical and financial restrictions, trading places is a logical first step towards fully-fledged use of 'water ground' for urban developments. By trading places, spatial requirements and wishes can be realized in a cost-effective manner. Upgrading dilapidated boathouse moorings, redesigning currently ignored, but promising riversides and double use of land for agricultural functions is only just the beginning.

Expanding the urban fabric in three steps. Buoyant foundations allow for a rethinking of the traditional way in which cities expand. Design for Tokyo Bay by Waterstudio.

2020-2040: EXPANDING THE URBAN FABRIC

From 2020 onwards, the use of open water in inner cities and suburbs for the expansion of urban structures on buoyant foundations will be well-established. To a large extent, reference projects will have led to the crystallization of building regulations, insurance issues, financing methods and maintenance programmes. In 2020, the step will have been taken from simple functions to large-scale urban expansions on water.

Infrastructure such as utilities and roads, ecological structures and green spaces will form the backbone of the city. By expansion over water, connection to these types of main structures is an obvious step.

The perception of urban planners is already changing. Ten years ago, the general image of the concept of living on water did not reach any further than a boathouse on a jetty. These days, space is reserved in almost every new urban expansion for a number of modern water villas.

Ho Chi Min is realizing amphibian buildings in a marsh, floating houses are being built in the New Water Project in the Netherlands, which involves a previously-reclaimed piece of land being allowed to fill up with water again, and in the Thames Gateway in London, houses are being built in the flood zones.

Images of the KSNM island in Amsterdam taken in August 1974 and again after 26 years of development in May 2000. The urban design for the KNSM island is by Dutch architect Jo Coenen, who also designed the circular building at the end of the island. The two large housing complexes at the left are by German architects Hans Kollhoff and Christian Rapp (top) and Belgium architect Bruno Albert (middle).

In the next decade, the realization will have filtered through to urban designers that the main difference involved in building on water lies just in the foundations. Planning in terms of water ground areas can then be implemented along traditional process lines. Municipal development processes will then make urban expansion onto water a matter of course.

Locations for the First Expansions onto Water

The most obvious places for expanding the urban fabric onto water are, of course, the port districts. They are the breeding grounds for expanding urban fabric onto the water.

Ocean-going vessels have become larger and larger in the last 30 years, in the competition for the most economical logistics. Old ports in the city centre were not built to accommodate these larger ships, and the ports were relocated or expanded in the direction of open water.

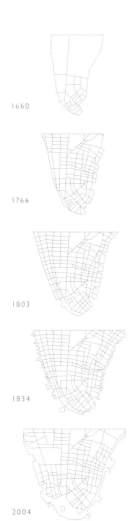

1660

1766

1803

1834

2004

Diagram showing the evolution of Lower Manhattan
from its humble beginning
as New Amsterdam in 1660
to a booming metropolis
in 2010.

This is a tremendous opportunity to develop former dock-lands. The price per square metre is particularly high in city centres. Dock areas are relatively large, with space on both water and land, and that makes them the ultimate location to increase the density of the city. The environmental aspects are another argument. Unfortunately, docklands are often contaminated. Filling in the ground hydraulically in the port is therefore not an option. Building on piles in the water also disturbs the polluted ground too much. Cleaning up is an op-tion, but is often very expensive.

Examples of cities that have seen ships withdraw from the old port are Liverpool, Dublin, Rotterdam, Amsterdam and Hamburg. In all these cases, the ports have relocated to areas outside the city. The old harbours have already undergone a facelift on land, where living, working and leisure activities have been fitted onto the quay. The spaces on water, however, are still unused.

Expanding urban fabric over the water is not new. If you compare the map of Manhattan, New York in 2010 with the map of 1660, and you follow the original waterfront, you will not find any water at all on the current map. A 250-m-wide border has been added to Lower Manhattan in the last three centuries. On the current street plan, the boundaries of the old island New Amsterdam can be recognized precisely. The planning history of New York is a succession of filling-in opera-tions, to meet the enormous demand for space in the city.

These large-scale land reclamation projects naturally had an effect on the current of the Hudson and could there-fore not be allowed to continue indefinitely. So the city admin-istration defined the furthest line for reclaiming land, and that became the definite boundary of Lower Manhattan. Floating buildings have a minimal effect on the current; not much more, at any rate, than the boat docks that fill the edges of Manhat-tan nowadays. Floating high-rise buildings or a buoyant expan-sion of the grid would be an interesting possibility. Floating parks would even kill two birds with one stone: not only would the water volume levels be maintained, they would also provide a new attractive waterfront. The Henry Hudson Parkway blocks any development on the waterfront at the moment, due to its situation alongside the water, but that would not cause a prob-lem. The sky-high price of land on Manhattan would also make it easy to create cost-effective floating buildings.

The following daring, but interesting idea goes one step further: by filling part of Central Park with buildings, a floating copy could be realized on the Hudson, on the west side of Manhattan, for a fraction of the cost. This would mean an upgrade of the waterfront and an enormous financial impulse and increase in density for the city. That will probably never happen. Thankfully – the park is far too important a part of the collective psyche of the city. But the economic and functional effects are nonetheless interesting eye openers.

2040-2100:
DYNAMIC CITIES

Urban structures have a longer lifespan than the programme of requirements on which they were based during their development. The first urban developments that will be built from 2020 onwards will therefore be ready for the first reconfiguration around 2040, in order to make room for the new urban landscapes that provide an answer to the spatial requirements of that moment. The result will be large floating districts, following the pattern of the existing city in their expansion, that can be relocated in due course with respect to each other or the mainland.

Dynamic cities. Cities like Amsterdam, New York or London are defined by their unique civic centres. Outside of this core the cities tend to be much more temporary, adapting and transforming to the needs of their inhabitants.

Building on water provides possibilities that reach further than floating architecture or a new approach to water management. It changes the whole perspective of city planning. Demographic, financial, social or political developments force city administrations to work continuously on the balance between the requirements of city dwellers and the urban environment. At the same time, the lifespan of city components is getting shorter. That is not so much true of the technical length of life, but more for the economic lifespan. The reason for this is the changing balance between the economic value of a building and the economic value of its location. In a growing city with increasing

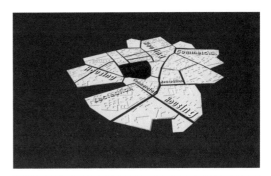

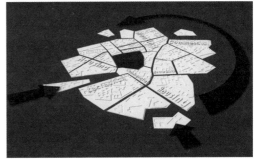

spatial pressure, the price of land in a central location rises faster than the material value of the building situated there. A common consequence is that a building in relatively good condition is demolished due to the development potential of the location. In the second half of the twenty-first century, an increasing number of buildings and functions will no longer be inextricably fixed to their location. By then, cities will form dynamic constellations, where buildings and functions can be moved throughout the duration of their life.

Buildings will no longer be demolished before they have reached the end of their technical life, just because the rising value of their location occasions it. The building can be relocated to a spot where the remaining economic value of the construction is more consistent with the value of the

THE FLOATING CITY CAN ONLY BE REALISED ONCE THE DOGMA OF THE STATIC CITY HAS BEEN ABANDONED

location. The building can then serve out the rest of its technical lifespan. This can provide savings on a large scale, in financial, ecological and energy terms. A building ceases to be immoveable property then; it becomes a product. Just like a car, a boat or a piano.

In the contemporary discussion about durability, the focus is one-sided and aimed at the reduction of CO_2 emissions. As a result, efforts in the area of durability are dominated by research into energy-saving processes and the reuse of materials. That is, of course, splendid and very necessary, but the gains in this area are partly cancelled out by the changing and unpredictable requirements of city dwellers.

Attention needs to be focussed once again on the flexibility of urban structures and components. Durability can then be achieved purely and simply by allowing components and structures to serve out their lifespan.

Shifting floating buildings onto the water and building buoyant urban components is technically feasible. Thirty years from now, dynamic urban development on city water will be normal. By then, cities will have expanded more than 20 per cent onto the water. At the same time, they will have given back a small part of the previously developed land to nature. That is hybrid urban design: a shift in the city from land to water. There is still a quarter of a century to work out the legal and planning conditions.

2100 AND BEYOND: MOVEABLE CITIES

Urbanization, the migration of country dwellers to the big city, means growth for the metropolises. However, this growth does not take place evenly. Some metropolises grow faster than others and even shrinkage is a scenario in some regions, in former East Germany, for instance.[8] For cities with a heart, soul and history, such as Amsterdam, New York or London, growth and even shrinkage is not really a problem.

The core of these cities has been defined for centuries. Everything that takes place around the core is less important and has a limited effect on the image of the city. In these cultural cities, the suburbs serve as a sort of functional application to allow the city as a whole to operate. The residential neighbourhoods, business parks, industrial areas and places for relaxation have a much more temporary character than the city centre. For the urban design structure of single-function cities with a less obvious centre, such as Silicon Valley in the USA and a number of large, new cities in China, shrinkage and growth will have a much more significant effect.

Consumption Urbanism

Cities have always reacted to changes in society, and it is important that they continue to do so. But in 100 years' time, the changes will have passed the historical city centres by. The centres that form an essential part of the character of the metropolis will be preserved. The water in and around these centres will become a location for living, working and leisure. A century from now, moveable city components will be a fact. The soul of the city will still live on in the old, static core, but liveability and functionality will come from the urban applications.

While cities on the water can grow or shrink for whatever reason, single-function, floating city components can become a consumer product. Moving a residential neighbourhood with several hundred houses, a few square kilometres of shopping centre, buoyant business parks and leisure in the form of floating sports facilities is possible. Cities consist of static centres surrounded by dynamic, floating city applications, which follow the growth regions and leave the shrinking regions.

Moveable Cities are Technologically Feasible

There are no technological restrictions on moving urban components over thousands of kilometres. That sounds incredible, but in the offshore and leisure industries, for instance, it is considered completely normal that cruise ships with thousands of residents change their location daily over water, or that floating oil production islands with hundreds of inhabitants are towed all over the world. Moving water homes over a distance of hundreds of kilometres has been taking place with great regularity in the Netherlands for years as well. These concepts are nearly all part of tried and tested technologies. However, ideas about the floating city can only be realized once there has been a change in perception about the dogma of the static city.

Expansion of cities 'beyond the waterfront', as sketched in this scenario for the future, is still in its infancy. But it offers undeniable opportunities for a new type of density and flexibility, and above all, a financial boost to urban development. This financial component lends credibility to the four process steps. No-one has a crystal ball. But extrapolation of existing technological expertise, for example by applying offshore technology to the building industry, makes the chance of urban growth on the water a real possibility.

Mobile cities. There are no technological restrictions on moving urban components over thousands of kilometres.

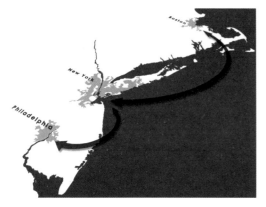

BUILDIN

NG ON V

WATER

The Eiffel Tower in Paris.

Chapter 3

TECHNOLOGY LEAP

The world around us does not seem to need explanation. The things people observe with their senses are categorized into concepts by their powers of comprehension. A building with a pointed roof is a house; a metal machine on four wheels is a car. That is how an apparently formless and chaotic world is turned into a series of recognizable phenomena. However, it also encourages the creation of prejudices and well-trodden paths: humans are always inclined to recognize things in their surroundings that they have already mentally pigeonholed. Someone standing in the middle of the Parc du Champs de Mars in Paris, trying to explain his whereabouts to someone on the telephone, will say that he is near the Eiffel Tower, not that he is close to the École Militaire. Although that particular complex at the other end of the Champs de Mars is much older and larger.

Humans reduce everything around them to easily recognizable images, to icons, because it is a way of understanding the world and a requirement for communicating with others. There is no communication without clichés. Advertisers love to make use of icons, in the shape of famous people or well-known places. They appeal to a broad public, who associate the icons with their corresponding values. The Eiffel Tower and the Empire State Building symbolize romance, the Capitol and the Palace of Westminster display power, Le Corbusier's chaise longue and Mies van der Rohe's Barcelona chair represent good taste.

A *terp* is an artificially created hill or mound to construct buildings on, protecting inhabitants from flooding and high tides. The practice of creating artificial hills was essential to the creation of modern-day Holland. On the photos a farm on a *terp* in the foreland of the river IJssel near Angerlo, before and after flooding of the foreland.

Inventors distinguish themselves from other people by their ability to think in concepts that do not yet exist. For someone who allows himself the freedom to think outside the box, the world is not a collection of clichés but a series of unique phenomena, each requiring its own approach. That is why inventors are often not understood to begin with: people are simply not capable of thinking outside their own preconceptions. Furthermore, to quote the Flemish poet Willem Elschot: 'Between dream and deed, laws stand in the way and practical concerns.'

Once these laws and practical concerns have been overcome, a seemingly unimportant discovery can lead to a significant change in society. In the Netherlands, for example, one such technological development was the windmill used to drain polders (reclaimed land enclosed by dikes). The Dutch used it to transform uninhabitable terrain into building ground and agricultural land. Centuries of diligent land-winning allowed them to turn low-lying swamps into a habitable, artificial system. This was achieved solely by thinking outside the box: if the natural habitat is not suitable for living in, you make it suitable. The *terp* (artificial dwelling mound), the dike and the polder made artificial Holland possible.

Jan Adriaanszoon Leeghwater, a Dutch mill-builder and hydraulic engineer who lived from 1575 to 1650, went down in history as the man who – together with a few others – was the pioneer of the large-scale drainage of the Netherlands. Based on sound commercial enterprise, he drained the Beemster and Purmer inland seas at the beginning of the seventeenth century and, in so doing, put the Netherlands on the map as a nation capable of creating its own land under sea level.

A less-known inventor who had an important influence on the development of the Netherlands was Cornelis Corneliszoon, a farmer from Uitgeest, who invented the crankshaft round 1592. Nowadays, the crankshaft is an essential component of almost all diesel and petrol engines. It converts the back-and-forward movement of the pistons into the rotating motion of the wheels. The crankshaft consists of a round pole with one or more projections (crankpins) on top, which are connected to the moving pistons via a rod. When the piston moves, the crankpin is pushed away and the crankshaft rotates. The first practical application of Corneliszoon's invention was in a sawmill, and there the conversion was exactly the reverse: from the rotating movement of the sails of the mill to the back-and-forward movement of the saw.

Corneliszoon was awarded a patent for the sawmill on 15 December 1593 and on 6 December 1597 for the crankshaft as a separate component. While he was developing the crankshaft, he already had the timber sawmill in mind: his

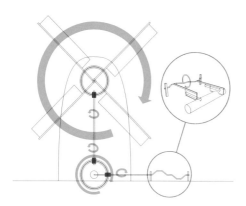

drawings of the first mill with crankshaft have been preserved. In 1594, Corneliszoon built his first timber sawmill, called Het Juffertje, a small mill that floated on a raft. In 1595, the mill was sold and relocated to Alkmaar. Because of the crankshaft, the mill suddenly worked 30 times faster than had been possible sawing by hand. Furthermore, sawing by machine was much more precise than by hand. As a result, the Dutch East India Company and the Dutch West India Company – the world's first multinationals – were able to build ships much more quickly than their competitors, kingdoms such as England and Spain, which led to a rapid growth in wealth and power. Corneliszoon died around 1607, but in spite of the tremendous importance of his invention, he is hardly known these days, not even in the Netherlands.

The original purpose of the crankshaft, designed by Cornelis Corneliszoon, was to convert the circular movement of windmills into a back-and-forth motion. This device allowed for the creation of wind-powered sawmills and helped to minimize manual labour within the industry.

As is often the case in history when an important technological invention is thwarted because it forms too large a threat to vested interests, Leeghwater made sure that Corneliszoon's crankshaft was hardly put into use at all during his lifetime. In his time, Leeghwater was held in high regard. He had a good relationship with the nobility, who were making huge profits in the new polders by the sale of new land; they had splendid country houses built there where they spent the summer months. Leeghwater knew Cornelis Corneliszoon personally, but the invention of the crankshaft was not in his best interests; he had his own windmill system which he used to drain the polders. He used his influence and power to ensure that no-one would make use of the patent on the crankshaft during Corneliszoon's lifetime. Only after his death did the sawmill industry begin to utilize his invention and to prosper as a result.

Viewed on its own, the crankshaft was a modest invention, but it made the Republic of Seven United Netherlands into one of the richest and most powerful nations in the world in the Dutch Golden Age. Naturally, there were countless other

IF THE NATURAL HABITAT IS NOT SUITABLE FOR LIVING IN, YOU MAKE IT SUITABLE

factors involved that determined the success of the Netherlands in the seventeenth century. But the invention of the crankshaft was one of the most important. There are historians who claim that Leeghwater's boycott of the crankshaft delayed the start of the Dutch Golden Age by around 15 years.

VERTICAL CITY – BUILDING IN THE AIR

Throughout history, there has always been pressure to increase density in the urban landscape. City centres are an enormous magnet for living and working. Until the mid-nineteenth century, cities remained relatively low. Building work took place close to the ground; living in towers was not an option.

Just as the invention of the polder drainage mill had consequences for spatial development in the Netherlands, other inventions formed the basis for large developments in urban design. Great technological leaps can often be traced to a single small invention.

One inventor who changed the appearance of the world and whose name is known everywhere is the American Elisha Otis. Sure enough: from the Otis lifts. Lifts had been in existence before Elisha Otis's time, but he was the man who introduced the first lift with a safety device in 1854 at the Crystal Palace in New York. The system worked with toothed guide rails in the lift shaft. The moment the pressure of the lift cable falls in the event of the cable breaking, claws in the lift cabin latch onto the rail and prevent the lift from falling, so that the cabin does not plunge downwards. Otis made the spectators in the Crystal Palace tremble by stepping into the monster himself, about 10 m above the ground, and subsequently giving the command to cut through the cable on which the construction was hanging. After only a few centimetres, the construction came to a standstill. His revolutionary new idea had worked. 'All safe, gentlemen!' he is said to have called triumphantly.

On 23 March 1857, the first Otis safety lift was installed. The honour went to the five-storey Haughwout Building on 488 Broadway in New York, designed by architect John P. Gaynor. Elisha Otis died only four years later at the age of 50, but his company continued to grow rapidly under the management of his sons. Within a few years, more than 2,000 buildings had been equipped with lifts. In 1889, the Eiffel tower opened, equipped with Otis safety lifts. In 1902, the 27-storey Flatiron Building followed, in 1912 the 60-storey Woolworth Building and in 1931 the 102-storey Empire State building, all three located in New York. This exponential increase in the number of storeys was not just made possible by

Elisha Otis introduces the first lift with a safety device in 1854 at the Crystal Palace in New York. His rethinking of the existing elevator added a mechanized failsafe in the unfortunate event that the elevator cable would snap. This forever changed the height restrictions associated with elevator travel, and allowed the skyscraper to become an active part of the architectural language.

Opening in January 2010, the Burj Khalifa in Dubai is currently the world's tallest building, at a staggering 828 m from the bottom to the tip of spire. In addition to breaking numerous height records, the building currently holds a few other world records, including the fastest elevators, which can reach speeds of 64km/h (40 mph).

the invention of electricity and the possibilities for increasing water pressure, but also and especially by the invention of the safety lift. It made it possible for people to ascend a large number of storeys quickly, without having to climb endless flights of stairs.[9]

In this way, a relatively modest invention radically changed the appearance of the big city for all time. The vertical city is something that goes without saying nowadays. The principle of the skyscraper is intact and is only improved on, by reaching increasingly higher into the air. At the moment, the Burj Khalifa in Dubai with its 828 m is the highest building in the world. Naturally, the building has the world's highest lift installation, but the lifts are also the fastest on earth. With a capacity of 21 people each, they carry visitors upwards at a speed of 64.8 km/h (18 m/s). By building ever higher, cities can continue to achieve higher density. It is not unthinkable that what seemed impossible only a few decades ago, could be realized somewhere on earth within a few years: a skyscraper I km high.

Pyramid City

The design presented in 2004 for Pyramid City, also known by the name Shimizu Mega-City Pyramid, goes one step further than the Burj Khalifa. The American architecture firm Bini Systems and the construction company Shimizu from Tokyo designed a complete city in Tokyo Bay in the shape of a pyramid. The pyramid, which would cover 4 km^2 at the base and rise to a height of 730 m, would be 14 times higher than the Great Pyramid at Giza. The colossus would consist of an open strut construction of megatrusses made from carbon nanotubes. Bini and Shimizu designed the project to cater for the enormous shortage of space in the Greater Tokyo Area. The idea shows some similarities with the design for the Tyrell Corporation pyramid, which comes into view several times in the 1982 science-fiction film *Blade Runner*.

Although the design was a serious proposal, and a documentary on the Discovery Channel in the series *Extreme Engineering* stated rather casually that the pyramid could be completed in 2110, it is not really likely that a construction like this could be realized within the foreseeable future. At any rate, Shimizu has put aside the plans, because the

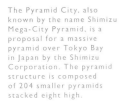

The Pyramid City, also known by the name Shimizu Mega-City Pyramid, is a proposal for a massive pyramid over Tokyo Bay in Japan by the Shimizu Corporation. The pyramid structure is composed of 204 smaller pyramids stacked eight high.

current state of technology does not allow for a construction like this. However, that does not take away from the fact that a design like this opens people's eyes to what could be possible, besides the one-dimensional skyscraper.

Sitting 1,000 m in height, with a total floor area of 800 hectares, Sky City 1000 is a superstructure comprised of 14 concave aerial bases referred to as 'space plateaus' stacked vertically. Although impossible to construct at the time of creation, it has been speculated that a structure of this magnitude could be physically built in the next 20 years.

Sky City 1000

Another design proposal that has its own Discovery Channel documentary in the *Extreme Engineering* series is Sky City 1000, also originating from Japan and intended to solve the space problem in Tokyo. The enormous construction company Takenaka came up with the design for a 1-km-high building as long ago as 1989. The skyscraper, with a 400-m-wide base, would consist of 14 so-called 'space plateaus' that would be stacked on top of each other and become increasingly narrow towards the top. Although the design is already more than 20 years old, it is just possible that the world's first 1-km-high tower will resemble the design for the Sky City 1000, in terms of its platform structure.

Each plateau in Sky City 1000 contains greenery in its centre with the residential units being placed on the periphery of the plateaus.

Otis probably never realized how far he had shifted the boundaries of the space suitable for building in the city. At the moment they happen, inventions are sometimes far removed from everyday reality. Building in the air goes without saying these days. Every city that wishes to achieve greater density and prestige will ensure that ever-higher skyscrapers are built.

DOUBLE-DECKER CITY – BUILDING IN THE GROUND

The lift is not the only invention that has radically changed the appearance of the city for all time. Another boundary demolished by new technology was the space under the city. It is impossible to imagine London now without the 'Tube'. If the Underground is out of use for a day, city life is totally disrupted. That fact became painfully clear during the terror-ist attacks in London on 7 July 2005. The British capital was startled during the morning rush hour by four bomb explo-sions. Three explosions took place in the underground within 30 minutes, there was one more on a double-decker bus half an hour later. There were 52 deaths. At a rough estimate, 700 people were injured, of whom 22 seriously.

To begin with, the authorities in London thought that the underground had been hit by a serious power failure. That came about because large power peaks had been noticed in the electricity net. After the bomb went off in the vicinity of Tavistock Square, it was very quickly clear to the outside world that a terrorist attack had taken place here. After the bombings, all the underground lines were immediately closed.

Well over 10 hours after the attacks, London was still in the throes of a huge traffic chaos. The underground network was still at a complete standstill on Thursday evening and bus transport started up again very slowly.

Millions of commuters were only able to reach their homes with the utmost difficulty. Many of them did not manage to get home at all and had to look for a hotel. For others, there was nothing else for it but to walk home. Car traffic was not back to anything like normal in the evening, either. Many roads and streets were still closed in the centre of this city with more than a million inhabitants, which led to other streets becoming totally blocked. Ship owners on the Thames carried stranded travellers free on their river tour boats. The underground did not start running again until the following day.[10]

(Left)
Map of the London Underground, one of the most famous subway systems in the world.

(Right)
Newspaper headlines at Waterloo station around 15.00 hours on 7 July 2005.

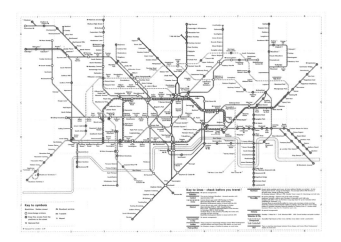

The London Underground has a reputable history. The Metropolitan Railway, now part of the Underground, was opened as the world's first underground system in phases from January 1863 and ultimately linked the city's most important railway stations. The technology spread quickly throughout Europe and later in the USA and other parts of the world. Nowadays the Underground has 270 stations and 400 km of railway tracks in total. That means it is still the longest in the world, in terms of total length.

Although the creation of the Tube is not linked to the name of a single individual, its invention had a far-reaching effect on the appearance and the experience of the world's cities. Just as lifts allowed cities to grow upwards, the underground added a whole new dimension beneath the city as it had existed up until then: a well-organized network of trains and tunnels that achieved direct connections between districts that had previously been far removed from each other. As a result, the density of the city could grow exponentially. Underground tunnel connections, however, can be much more than just a network of railway tracks, as is illustrated by the tunnels under Montreal and Houston.

Underground City Montreal

Building under the ground is not just a response to lack of space. The climate can also be a reason for putting buildings and public life under the ground. The Canadian city of Montreal is the setting of the largest underground complex in the world: the Underground City Montreal, known locally by the name Réso. The Réso consists of a series of mutually connected complexes in the city centre, both above and under the ground, and has given the city its nickname Double-Decker City.

The tunnels have a total length of 32 km and are spread over an area of 12 km². They connect not just various

Map of the Underground City of Montreal, an interwoven series of tunnels in the city's centre, connecting the subway system with commercial, residential and business spaces.

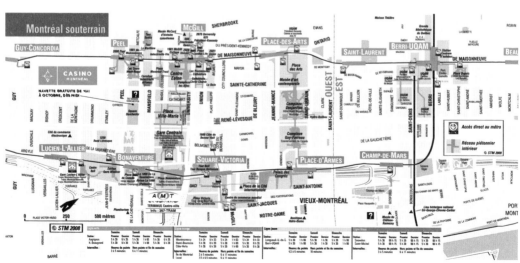

underground stations and buildings, but are also liveable spaces in their own right. They have more than 120 entrances, are air-conditioned and the lighting is just as good as in buildings above ground. Most of them have shops on both sides. In the winter, when it can be freezing cold in Montreal, more than 500,000 people make use of the underground city every day.

Downtown Houston Tunnel System

While the underground system in Montreal works well mainly because it is too cold above ground in the winter for a pleasant stay, the inhabitants of Houston are looking for a way to cool down in the summer in their under-ground tunnels. The Houston Tunnel System consists of a network of air-conditioned tunnels approximately 6 m below street level with a total length of 10 km. It links 95 downtown city blocks, but for many people it is a travel desti-nation in its own right: all sorts of shops and restaurants can be found there. Every day 150,000 people make use of it, especially when it is raining or when the summer temperature approaches 40 degrees Celsius above the ground.

The Houston Tunnel System is a series of above- and below-ground tunnels that keep the downtown inhabitants out of the harsh summer sun.

Amfora

In the twenty-first century, building underground is also being investigated as a serious alternative; in the Netherlands by organizations such as the Centre for Underground Building, a collaboration between more than 100 enterprises, govern-ment agencies and knowledge centres. Various designers show that much is possible in this area. In 2009 the Dutch architec-ture firm Zwarts & Jansma and construction company Struk-ton came up with the Amfora plan, a proposal for an enor-mous underground city beneath the canals of Amsterdam.

Amsterdam is bursting at the seams: space is limited and the narrow streets are often completely blocked with traffic. Amfora (which stands for Alternative Multifunctional Underground Space Amsterdam) is intended to solve

the space problem with a 50 km long network of tunnels under the canals in the centre. There will be space for parking garages, shops and relaxation facilities, including cinemas and other places of entertainment that do not need much daylight. The plans also propose directing all the motor traffic below street level: immediately after leaving the Amsterdam ring road, all traffic would drive into the tunnels.

Amfora is intended to solve Amsterdam's space problems with a 50 km long network of tunnels under the canals in the centre. All the motor traffic is directed below street level.

It is not very likely that this design will ever be realized. It is too large-scale and the old centre of Amsterdam is too vulnerable. But the lively discussions that were provoked in the media and the city administration by the design when it was presented in 2009 make it clear that a visionary plan can offer a solution to urgent problems, and that concrete images can lead to great enthusiasm, even in politicians and inhabitants who were sceptical at first.

Amfora Amstel, developed by Strukton and designed by Zwarts & Jansma Architects, is a plan to expand Amsterdam's historic centre through the development of multifunctional facilities under the city's canals. The six-storey urban expansion would increase local residential comfort by being a mixed use structure housing lecture-halls, cinemas and concert halls, tennis courts, a fitness centre, an entertainment centre, a shopping centre and parking lots.

BEYOND THE WATERFRONT –
BUILDING ON WATER

High-rise buildings and the Underground are normal components of every large city these days. They are an integral part
of the concept most people now have of urban space. But a few
centuries ago they were just ideas, which turned the image of
the city that had existed until then upside down. Building on
water will most likely have the same effect. At the moment
this does not fit in with existing concepts about the functioning of the city, but in just a few decades it could be completely
absorbed into the city dweller's perception of his or her
own environment.

History of Floating Objects

The innovations that lie at the basis of buoyant foundations
are quite old. The first forms of living on water were rafts
with huts on them, followed by wooden houseboats and
barges. Later versions had a steel understructure but retained
the disadvantage of maintenance. Wooden and steel houseboats and barges have to pay regular visits to the boatyard
for maintenance, usually every five years.

The most important innovation in the field of floating
foundations is the invention of reinforced concrete. Reinforced
concrete is a combination of concrete and steel bars. The bars
are added to the places where tension will occur. The French-
man Joseph Monier acquired a patent for this process in 1867. It
is possible to reinforce concrete with steel because the coeffi-
cient of thermal expansion for steel is the same as for concrete.

Using reinforced concrete, caissons could be made
that were placed under the houseboats as floating foundations.
These concrete foundations require far less maintenance,
provided the covering of concrete on the steel reinforcement
is sufficient. The quality of these foundations is so high that
most houseboats are equipped with them these days.

The new vision on floating urban developments has led
to the requirement for larger buoyant foundations. In the last
few years, new patents have been registered for this type
of construction. The patent for a sandwich construction of
prefabricated concrete and polystyrene foam has opened the
way for floating city islands a few hundred square metres in

size. The same urban functions can be realized on these islands as on solid ground. Housing, roads and green areas can have the same size and appearance as they do now in existing cities.

Diagram of the composition of buoyant concrete. Rather than using the traditional combination of concrete, steel and polystyrene foam, this lightweight concrete alternative will have the ability to be a standalone material.

Floating Solid Foundation

The development of floating foundations is in full swing. The current generation of buoyant foundations is actually rather primitive. Concrete, steel and polystyrene foam: these materials have been used for decades already and have proved themselves with regard to buoyancy and maintenance. But they are far from ideal. Costs, processing, appearance, weight and strength can all be improved further.

The Dutch company Dutch Docklands has a patent on large floating foundations and is currently working on the development of buoyant aerated concrete. This concrete is lighter than water (400 g per litre), but as yet misses the strength required to do service as a floating foundation. Furthermore, for the production of large blocks the warming effect during the hardening stage is not yet ideal. The costs of the material are still considerably higher than concrete and polystyrene and the load possibilities are not as good as traditional floating foundations. But lightweight floating solids still have tremendous potential. Imagine for a moment: you make a mould fairly simply on the floor of a dry dock, you fill up the mould with lightweight concrete, you let water flow into the dry dock and your floating foundation is ready.

The holy grail of buoyant foundations is easy to describe. It is light and easy to produce using material that can be obtained cheaply all over the world; it is strong, will not be damaged by salt water, is simple to process and above all, can be shaped into a large platform without using other materials. Floating solids made from synthetic material, with the same rigidity and structure as human bones, could be the ultimate material for foundations.

EXISTING BUILDING BLOCKS FOR FLOATING CITIES

Floating cities may seem like a dream for the future, but the components required have been available for some time in other fields. The only thing that is needed is a new vision on what is already present. In industrial building and the offshore industry there are already many examples of floating products. They can provide inspiration for the design of floating city components. We review several of them here to gain an idea of the current state of the technology.

Floating Office Building

Images of the Bonte Zwaan, a floating office building, before and after its 2002 renovation.

In the Houthavens in Amsterdam, there is a three-storey floating office building. The boat was built in 1966 at the NDSM shipbuilders as a floating office building for Vrachtmail, a subsidiary of the KNSM, the Royal Dutch Steamship Company. In 1980, the building was taken over by the AMVV, the association of professional seamen, who gave it the name Bonte Zwaan, which means Colourful Swan. The building was subsequently used as a centre for inland shipping. The central feature was the shipping exchange, surrounded by facilities such as chartering broker's offices, a shop and bank branch. The building also took on an important social function for the bargemen with facilities such as childcare and a nursery school, an office for social and legal advice, library, laundrette, canteen, cinema and party centre. In 2002, De Bonte Zwaan was converted into a floating office building and these days it houses the studios of fashion designers, architecture firms and other creative designers.

Floating Prison

In the Netherlands, the demand for prison cells fluctuated considerably in the first decade of this century. A cell surplus turned into a shortage. A floating prison, designed by Royal Haskoning and built in Zaandam, meant that the link between location and function was removed, which made it easier to react to demand. The fact that the Dutch Justice  system was prepared to invest in a concrete caisson indicates their very strong faith in its functioning, safety and durability. New York has also had a floating gaol in the Hudson for years and years, called the Vernon C. Bain Center.

Floating High-Rise Buildings

In 2001, the salvage and transport giant Mammoet van Seumeren was responsible for a wonderful spectacle in Rotterdam. A ten-storey office building was built in a hangar and was subsequently moved a few dozen miles over water to Schiedam, taking three days for the journey. During transportation, the tower stood on a floating foundation. Once it arrived at its destination, the building was hoisted onto its ultimate foundations on land.

Floating Airport

In overcrowded Japan, floating airports have already been built on artificial islands in the sea, such as Kansai International Airport near Osaka. The floating airport is a much cheaper solution because no land has to be drained to build it, according to Hachiro Yamaichi of the 'Mega-Float' consortium, where the companies participating include Mitsubishi Heavy Industries and Sumitomo Heavy Industries. Furthermore, the floating runways are earthquake-proof

and environmentally friendly. A prototype intended for a series of tests was moored in waters near Tokyo in 1999 and dismantled a year later, after the trials were completed.

Floating Parking Garage

In Monaco every square metre is worth its weight in gold. Double use of land is the rule rather than the exception. A floating dock built to expand Condamine Harbour functions as a parking garage for 400 vehicles and also as a breakwater and mooring space for cruise ships 200 m in length. It was built in Spain by a consortium of Spanish builders, commissioned by the government of Monaco. The move to Monaco took almost two weeks. The floating jetty has a draught of 14 m and was attached to the seabed with fixed anchor chains in the more than 50-m-deep harbour. The dock is secured to the quay by means of a moveable entrance. The dock also provides extra mooring berths for speedboats; that is naturally almost a necessity in Monaco.

Floating Road

The longest floating bridge in the world is the 2,285-m-long Evergreen Point Floating Bridge in Lake Washington, Seattle. The bridge, which was opened on 28 August 1963, was not the first floating bridge on the lake. That honour goes to the Lake Washington Floating Bridge, which was the largest floating construction in the world at the time it was built in

1940. The Evergeen Point Bridge was designed to carry 65,000 vehicles a day, but these days around 115,000 vehicles use the bridge to cross the lake every day. The heavy load has meant that the bridge is reaching the end of its lifespan; the Washington State Department of Transportation is currently working on a new floating bridge that should be in operation in 2014.

Passenger Ships

Floating cities have existed for more than a hundred years: in the guise of cruise ships. The largest cruise ship in the world

Images of Royal Caribbean's Oasis of the Seas. Currently the largest ship in the world, being twice as large as the Titanic, its unique design accommodates a large open garden in its centre flanked by two parallel apartment blocks. Due to this layout, there are no staterooms without a window.

at the moment is the Oasis of the Seas owned by the shipping company Royal Caribbean International. The ship can accommodate a total of 6,296 passengers and 2,165 crew: the size of a small village. The ship, which had its maiden voyage on 5 December 2009, is 360 m long and its displacement is approximately 100,000 tons. That makes the vessel twice as large as the Titanic, which had a displacement of 52,000 tons. In the middle of the ship is 'Central Park', an enclosed garden with more than 12,000 plants and 56 trees. Views over the garden are provided from the Rising Tide Bar, which can move up and down over a height of three decks.

Production Platforms

Many building elements found in offshore technology can be applied in floating buildings. Drilling rigs are particularly interesting: enormous steel or concrete structures for the extraction of oil and/or gas, which can be relocated over large distances over water and where dozens of people can be housed long-term. They are found as fixed platforms on columns in shallow water up to a depth of around 600 m, and in floating versions for deep waters. The floating versions are found in various forms, including tension-leg platforms and semi-submersibles. Tension-leg platforms are floating platforms held in place with long 'tendons' resting on the seabed. The deepest platform of this type is at a water depth of 1,432 m. Semi-submersible platforms are platforms on columns that rest on several separately positioned pontoons. The whole construction is submerged to the point where the pontoons are underwater and only the columns stick up through the water line. Semi-submersibles are attached to the seabed by means of suction anchors: hollow poles with a closed upper side that are placed on the seabed and subsequently vacuum pumped. As long as the vacuum remains intact, they can resist extreme upwards thrusts.

Oil and gas drilling platform in the Pacific Ocean.

Floating Fortresses

There are sea forts in various places in the world and their construction closely resembles oil platforms: they are moved

to their location on floating pontoons that are subsequently sunk to the seabed. The Maunsell Sea Forts, for instance, which were sunk into the Thames and Mersey Estuaries during the Second World War to defend Great Britain. After the war they fell into disuse; a few are still standing. In the mid-1960s, several of the forts were used by pirate radio stations.

The remains of the Maunsell Sea Forts look dilapiated these days, but the plans for floating sea forts are very much alive. In March 2010 it was announced that the Pentagon's Defense Advanced Research Projects Agency (also known as DARPA) is carrying out research into self-assembling, modular floating platforms, built up from standard sea containers. Each container would be given a specific function, such as living quarters, command cells, communications shacks or weapons stations. As soon as they have been deployed into the water from a cargo ship, the modules, which are driven by small propeller blades, group themselves into larger units using navigation computers.[12]

The Maunsell Sea Forts dotting the Thames and Mersey estuaries.

NEW PRODUCTS FOR GROWING METROPOLISES

At the moment, the Netherlands are at the forefront of developments in floating building blocks. Various committees of architects, engineers, hydraulic engineers and policy-makers are working together on the development of new buoyant products. Architects and developers see the need for raising the level of the market for floating buildings. At this higher level there is no longer a difference with buildings on land in terms of quality, comfort and lifespan. In this way, expanding the urban fabric onto water can take place fully and satisfactorily.

80 COUNTRIES HAVE SERIOUS PROBLEMS WITH CLEAN WATER

As discussed in Chapter 1, maintaining the infrastructure is one of the greatest challenges for growing metropolises worldwide. Mobility, water and energy supplies, food provision and environment are the fundamental issues in maintaining liveability levels in the city. Building across the boundary between land and water can also provide new solutions.

Mobility

In many metropolises, mobility is one of the biggest problems. In Bombay, for example, the pressure exerted by urbanization on the infrastructure leads to daily increasing congestion. The roads have a hard time of it and get jammed under the influence of the steadily increasing stream of traffic. There is an enormous need for increased road capacity, partly because of the fast-growing economy, but there is no room in the existing city. That is why urban designers in Bombay are seriously investigating the possibilities for floating roads. Floating motorways on water, on both sides of the peninsula, could ease the traffic build-up.

One big problem for floating roads that still needs to be solved is stability. For the type of water areas as found in Bombay, with heavy seas and a strong current, a semi-submersible highway could be a possibility. That is a motorway built high above the water on piles supported by a floating underwater foundation. As a result, the waves have hardly any influence on the road, which improves stability and safety. Ships can even cross these roads because the buoyant elements do not have to be completely continuous. A floating road from Gibraltar to Morocco is also a possibility with the introduction of the semi-submersible highway.

Semi-submersibles consist of large pontoons floating just under the surface of the water with narrow columns jutting out above the water to support a platform at a considerable height above the surface of the water. Due to the fact that the hull construction is submerged and the water line is only transected by narrow columns, the semi-submersible experiences far less disturbance from the pressure of the waves than a normal ship. A semi-submersible is never completely under water.

The principle of semi-submersibles can also be applied to floating roads. These roads already exist on a small scale, are predominantly single lane and are used on the water for temporary purposes. However, roads on water in a more permanent form can provide relief for the traffic bottlenecks that plague almost every urban conurbation. Everything is possible: bypasses straight over the water, or motorways floating in rivers parallel to the river banks.

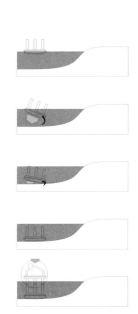

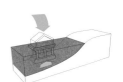

Two types of semi-submersibles. The first base structure rests on the sea floor (images 1-5). When the sea depth exceeds a certain depth, the base structure is a buoyant pontoon (images 6-8).

Water Supply

In many metropolises, the supply of fresh water is a problem. Only one to two per cent of the total amount of water in the world is fresh water. This supply is increasingly difficult to obtain and the costs of purification and delivery keep rising. Many large cities are expected to be faced with these

A semi-submersible highway designed by Waterstudio.

(Left)
Below waterline.

(Right)
Above waterline.

problems sooner or later. Mexico City, for example, is already contending with annual water shortages. It inspired the city administration to launch an advertisement campaign entitled 'February 2010: The City May Run Out of Water'. According to the World Bank, 80 countries have serious problems with clean water, with all the consequences that brings for public health and the economic production of these countries. Two billion people – around 40 per cent of the world's population – have no access to clean drinking water or sanitary facilities. [13]

The solution is to start producing fresh water on a large scale. In a number of countries in the Middle East this is already a daily activity. Large-scale desalination uses extremely large amounts of energy, making it very costly compared to the use of fresh water from rivers or groundwater. In a country where water is more expensive than petrol, this is acceptable for the time being. Not from an environmental perspective, of course.

The source for fresh water could be seawater. Large, luxury ships, which are intended for a long sojourn at sea, are already equipped with desalination installations these days. The product of the future that does not yet exist is a floating, self-sufficient fresh water production island. An island like this would have enough space to acquire solar energy to use for desalination. Technological processes to simplify desalination are in full swing all over the world. Scarcity of water will speed up the process and make it a smaller step towards achieving desalination on the open sea.

Energy

For years and years, energy consumption per head of the population has been rising worldwide. Economic growth in countries like India and China goes hand-in-hand with a considerable increase in energy consumption and a run on fossil fuel reserves. Cities will go in search of new independent sources of energy. That independence is of crucial importance. In the contemporary society, energy comes from far away. In the past, energy generation took place in your own house and was centred round the open fire and the water pump. History has shown that at a certain point it is logical to control the generation of energy and therefore to opt for centralization. In Western Europe gas is obtained these days through pipelines originating in Russia. The pipelines cross Ukraine. In 2008 it became clear that gas deliveries to Europe are dependent on political friction between these two countries. Now you can see the trend of investigating how energy can be generated locally again, perhaps even at house level. That is the direction the energy supply is going in. That is illustrated by solar cells and collectors, heat pumps and small windmills.

The most obvious form of energy generation on water is wind energy. The wind can reach high speeds on the open surfaces of the water and, besides that, large wind farms on water cause less nuisance than in densely-populated areas on land. Wind farms are already regularly utilized on a large scale on water, as a result. In the North Sea, for example, 23 km from the Dutch coast is the Princess Amalia Wind Farm, which became operational in 2008. The park has 60 wind turbines, capable of supplying 125,000 households with sustainable energy.

Designed by ONOFFICE, this speculative wind farm off the coast of Norway takes the traditional offshore windmill system and integrates habitable space within the design. Called Turbine City, the project mixes tourism and turbines, becoming a vessel to help the general public understand this renewable energy source.

The Zeekracht master plan by OMA is a strategic proposal for renewable energy production in the North Sea. The master plan proposes the creation of an Energy Super-Ring connecting existing and future offshore wind farms to create a constant source of renewable energy for the surrounding countries and those beyond. The industrial resources of surrounding nations are combined in Zeekracht's production belt, while a new reef system extends throughout the area to stimulate local marine ecosystems. The creation of an International Research Centre on site provides a shared platform for worldwide research and development of offshore renewable energy.

An innovative example is the design Zeekracht (Sea Power) presented by architecture firm OMA in 2009. Wind power from the North Sea can eventually supply just as much energy as the oil in the Persian Gulf now, was the statement made by OMA on that occasion. The plan proposes a ring of wind farms that connect the seven North Sea countries in a stable energy generation network. An international institute for renewable energy at the centre of the network would bring expertise together and symbolize the international collaboration. With the help of shared infrastructure and knowledge, the North Sea countries can achieve the reversal from fossil fuels to renewable energy; that is the hope, at any rate. By 2050, wind energy combined with solar energy could make Europe virtually independent of the oil states and Russia.

One of the biggest problems with wind farms at sea is maintenance. In the current situation, maintenance and repair work has to take place on open sea. So it would be natural to step over to floating wind farms. That would make it possible to tow the windmills from sea to land for maintenance, where work can be carried out under controlled circumstances. It sounds intensive but it is not so very different from the floating oil platforms that are towed all the way from Nigeria to the Netherlands for maintenance.

Another source of energy at sea is wave power. Water moves and is therefore a potential energy generator of inestimable size. Wave energy can be generated using fixed and floating installations. With a buoyant installation, use can be made, for example, of floats secured to a spindle with a neutral mechanism: when the float rises, it takes the spindle with it; when the float goes down again, it falls into neutral. One example of a fixed installation consists of a series of tapering channels (tapchans). When a wave flows into a channel, the temporarily raised water pressure propels part of the water into a reservoir situated at a higher level. From there, the water flows back to sea level through a turbine.

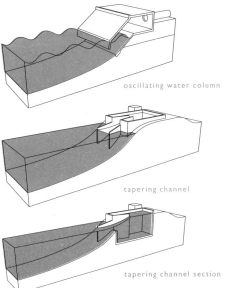

oscillating water column

tapering channel

tapering channel section

Two ways of energy extraction from wave power: the oscillating water column and the tapering channel.

Another method works with an oscillating water column. It makes use of a hanging airtight chamber with a valve half-submerged in water. As a wave enters the chamber, the air pressure increases so that air leaves the column via the valve. This flow of air then drives a turbine. A small power station (75 kW) using this principle is installed on the Scottish island of Islay.

An energy facility on water does not have to be confined to wind and wave power. The most promising developments are in the field of solar energy. Anyone who has ever spent a summer's day on a boat knows the power of the sun reflecting off the water. Floating solar cells are the most likely interpretation of this idea: floating platforms that move with the rhythm of the waves. The Swiss researcher Thomas Hinderling, CEO of the Centre Suisse d'Electronique et de Microtechnique, received 5 million US Dollars in 2008 from the Ras al Khaimah Emirate of the UAE to build a prototype in that country. He estimates that an island with a diameter of one mile can produce 190 megawatts. The break-even point

A design for floating solar blankets by Waterstudio. Hundreds of solar cells, each placed on a small conical buoy just above the water surface, form a chainmail of floating solar blankets. These floating solar fields provide a much higher yield than similar solar cells found on land. By being on water they are also self-cleaning.

lies at a price of 0.15 US Dollar per kilowatt hour, or twice the current price of electricity in the USA. The islands consist of a buoyant plastic membrane with mirrors to collect solar energy. The mirrors are used to convert liquid into steam, which can drive a turbine.[14]

A further step is the development of non-rigid floating solar blankets. In this system, thousands of solar cells, none larger than 1 m², are placed on a small conical buoy just above the water surface. Together they form a sort of chain mail: floating solar fields with a much higher yield than a similar number of solar cells on land. Sea water continuously washes over the solar cells because they are situated just above the surface of the water. Self-cleaning glass, already in use in houses, provides continuous cleaning of the cells.

Food

Due to the heavy pressure of urbanization on the country-side, there is little or no room around metropolises now for agricultural activities. At the same time, the demand for self-sufficiency and food production close to where customers are located is on the increase. For the sustainable city of the future to function well, urban farms would be a good solution.[15]

Vertical farms, like those suggested by the Dutch architecture firm MVRDV in the design proposal Pig City, provide an answer to space issues, but floating urban agriculture goes much further. Experiments are already being carried out with circular floating elements upon which plants are cultivated.

The problem that has to be solved is not so much cultivation on water, but harvesting the produce. How can that process be simplified? Our idea is that the farmer does not go to the crops, but that the crops come to the farmer. The ideal situation would look something like this: elongated floating platforms, built up from modules measuring 10 x 100 m that

To feed the entire Dutch population, MVRDV architects proposed the whole lifecycle of pig farming and production for meat to be contained within a vertical tower. This idea would minimize the use of the Dutch land for pig farming and minimize the transportation and environmental hazards currently plaguing the system.

resemble catamarans, with hollow tubes between which there are lightweight constructions a little like egg cartons. This will hold the fertile soil together. The tube construction provides buoyancy and stability and can be used for the transport and storage of fresh water if the floating agricultural land is situated on salt water. Because they are not tied to their location, the 'fields' can be relocated during the growing season. Their position in relation to the sun can also be adjusted.

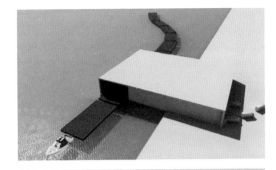

The method of harvesting is completely different from that on land. The modules are pulled to the harvesting location in an elongated chain, where the crops are then brought in off the land under efficient and controlled conditions. At the same time, the floating agricultural modules are made ready for a following cycle.

Environment

Pollution has made the quality of water a point of attention worldwide. Charles Moore, an American oceanographer, discovered the 'Great Pacific Garbage Patch' in 2008, a floating plastic 'soup' that stretches from 500 nautical miles off the Californian coast, over the northern Pacific, past Hawaii all the way to Japan. According to Moore, there are 100 million tons of flotsam drifting around, held in place by underwater currents.[16]

Module floating platforms, resembling catamarans, with a hollow-tube infrastructure, can provide floating agricultural fields. Harvesting is completed by pulling the individual modules in a chain to the offshore harvesting location. The crops are then gathered and distributed on land, while the floating agricultural modules are replanted and made ready for the following growth cycle. The cycle continues endlessly and can provide a local, year-round food source.

In order to prevent dead zones appearing in the oceans (linked areas where there is hardly any life because of pollution), the debris that has been dumped in the water for decades must be cleaned up. One way of achieving this would be the use of water vacuum cleaners. The vacuum cleaners would need to be self-sufficient in terms of energy, with solar energy as the most likely source. The cleaners look like gigantic jellyfish that suck up the water on the underside with flexible hoses. The inside surfaces of these hoses is

Diagram showing the extent of the ocean affected by the 'Great Pacific Garbage Patch'.

Lacking a brain and many of the systems associated with other living creatures (central nervous system, respiratory system, circulatory system), the jellyfish is a unique creature in the animal kingdom. Part of the Cnidaria phylum, jellyfish come in a variety of forms and styles connected by being composed of Mesoglea, a jelly-based structure that takes the place of traditional bones or exoskeleton systems.

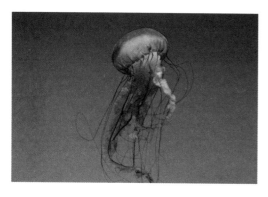

processed with a material to which the plastic debris adheres. The vacuum jellyfish is also completely flexible. The pump system works like a heart. The wave movements generate a peristaltic contraction that pulls the water through the hoses. These hoses work like coronary arteries that slowly get silted up. Once a hose is full – it can be as much as 100 m in length – it is closed off and remains as a compact string on the surface of the water. These hoses are simple to collect after which they can be used as raw materials for new products. Thousands of these jellyfish, each a few dozen metres in diameter, will probably have to be in operation for decades to reduce the size of the soup.

Another problem is the threat to biodiversity. Monoculture, genetic modification, erosion and climate change are responsible for the disappearance of plants and animals. The elongated atolls in the Pacific contain the most beautiful islands. A large number of atolls that rise less than a metre above sea level will disappear due to the rising water level. As a result, the fauna and flora will also be swallowed up by the water. To deal with this problem, animals and plants will have to be partly migrated in the future. That could be to higher-situated areas but could also be to a floating donor island. This donor island would consist of large buoyant foundations with a natural upper layer with the same geological structure as the original atoll. The donor islands would be moored to the island decades before the expected submersion, so that the vegetation would have the chance to gradually take possession of the floating island.

The Rangiroa atoll, located in French Polynesia, is known for growing pearl oysters and its robust reef systems. It is the largest atoll in the Tuamotus Archipelago, with local waters that contain a variety of exclusive fauna, making it a popular travelling destination for divers and tourists.

Ecological structures are also being driven into a corner because a growing number of earth dwellers is taking increasing possession of the limited space available on the planet. In places where biodiversity is threatened by humans, floating forests could provide a solution. At the moment low-height woods on relatively limited floating units are possible, but for large-scale afforestation, dozens of acres of large floating forests on salt water would be required. These mangrove-like woods would offer a home to flora and fauna in and close to extremely large urban expansions onto water. The challenge is to find buoyancy that does not collapse under the continually growing amount of biomass and that provides sufficient rigidity to allow taller trees to take root.

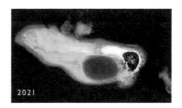

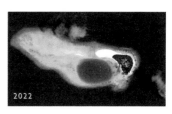

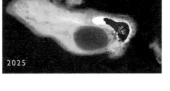

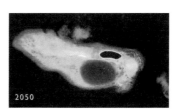

2020 – Original atoll.

2021 – Creation of a floating donor island extension begins.

2022 – Plant grow begins to develop on the donor extension.

2025 – Plants and trees continue to overtake the donor extension.

2030 – Extension completely overrun by vegetation.

2040 – Original island begins to flood, inhabitants begin to move to artificial donor island.

2050 – Original island completely flooded, floating donor island becomes a self sufficient entity.

A floating forest designed
by Waterstudio.

Changing Boundaries

The generally accepted boundaries of where it is possible to
build have been stretched again and again in the previous centuries. The boundary between land and water is one of the last
borders that can be demolished, after building in the air and
underground. But unlike high-rise and underground building,
building on water will have to gain greater credibility to be
accepted by the masses. The development of new products
has only just begun, but the concept of the floating city gives
architects and inventors a new playing field to provide growing
metropolises with solutions to burning issues in the spheres
of mobility, water, energy, food provision and the environment.
Most likely it will take a generation for the floating city to
become just as established as the vertical city, but by that time
the indispensability of water as an element of the space suitable
for building in the metropolis will be an undeniable fact.

FROM W

VATER C

ITY TO

HYDRO

CITY

A floating house underneath
the Hwy 99 Aurora Bridge
in Seattle, WA, USA.

Chapter 4

HYDROCITY

Living on water is a relatively new development in urban design. Very few architects and urban designers are involved with the subject fulltime. In this development phase, visions and innovations are not yet obstructed by regulations and conventions. It's just like Internet. In the beginning, its development was dependent on small groups of computer nerds, who together changed the world by constantly inventing new applications. When Microsoft founder Bill Gates proclaimed in the second half of the 1970s that his ambition was to get a personal computer on every desk in the world, that was a strange idea in the world view prevalent at that time. Now he is one of the richest men on earth and a world without the pc is impossible to imagine.

The brightly coloured
houses of an Inuit village
are sprinkled alongside the
mountainous snow-covered
landscape.

With the rise of living on water, ideas and images come into being that rouse the interest of many people because they are new. However, the prototype of the floating city does not yet exist. Many variants of living on water can be devised, each one providing a supplement to the existing city and an answer to a specific urban problem. The solitary floating city, one which functions self-sufficiently and completely separately from the fixed world with its own facilities in the open sea, is a utopia that will certainly not be realized for the time being, but does appeal to the imagination.

In the great majority of world cities, water is an important spatial element. It is no coincidence that most metropolises are situated on the water. In many of these cities, the presence of water was the reason for their foundation and their prosperity. Water, in the form of rivers or seas, was an important lifeline and increased the opportunities for trade and transport. In other words, water was of vital importance.

There are different types of water. Any sort of categorization is subjective and depends on the cultural background of the person determining the categories. The American linguists Edward Sapir and Benjamin Lee Whorf state in their hypothesis of linguistic relativity – in summary – that the language spoken influences the way in which people interpret the world. The Eskimos, or Inuit to give them their correct name, are known for the fact that they can describe dozens of different types of snow. In the same way, one form of water is not the same as another.

Different sorts of water have differing characteristics that influence the building possibilities. For instance, there are city canals, rivers, seas and lakes, canals, swamps and wet polders. There is fresh, brackish, salt, acidic and even alkaline water, each with a different effect on building materials (also called the 'aggression' of the water). There is stagnant and running water; there are places with large and places with small fluctuations in the water level. There is water with ice formation and drifting ice, water in a bay, an atoll or an archipelago. There is thick mire water, peat water and seepage water. All these types of water have different characteristics that determine the building possibilities, just as every type of subsoil on land has its own method of foundation.

Water cities can also be divided into various categories, in for instance waterfront cities, river cities, port cities, canal cities, archipelago cities and island cities. Needless to say, this subdivision is not rigorous. A city can have the characteristics of more than one type, but usually one specific feature dominates. Rotterdam, for example, is both a river city and a port city. But it is principally a port city because it is one of the largest ports in the world. Furthermore, water cities can change character in the course of time. Bangkok, for example, had a large number of canals (khlongs) up until the mid-nineteenth century, which would have given the city a high ranking in the list of canal cities. These days, however, almost all the khlongs have disappeared and Bangkok is principally a river city.

Port Cities

A port city derives its most important economic activities from the port industry. The spatial structure of the city follows a generally recognizable pattern. The port takes up most of the surface of the city and consists of a waterway with on either side a large number of increasingly finely-structured branches, comparable to the lungs of a living organism. The branches are built in such a way as to maximize the length of the quayside, which provides the maximum amount of space for the transhipment of goods.

Rotterdam, Antwerp and Hamburg are all good examples of this type of city. In the past, harbours were situated

in the old city centre, but the need for increasingly more space led to the ports being relocated to areas outside the city in the direction of the open sea, so that increasingly large ocean-going vessels with a deeper draught could put in. The old dock areas in the inner cities were subsequently freed up for new urban developments and became in many cases extremely desirable new city districts: 'Hafencity' in Hamburg, the 'Kop van Zuid' in Rotterdam, 'Het Eilandje' in Antwerp. By now, the pressure of urbanization can really be felt too in the former dock areas as well. The docklands have a limited surface area and there is plenty of water present. So it is not unthinkable that future urban developments in these areas could take place on instead of next to the water.

Panoramic view of the Botafogo Beach area in Rio de Janeiro, Brazil, located on the western shore of Guanabara Bay. The Sugarloaf Mountain peninsula, seen in the distance, protects the beach from the Atlantic Ocean.

Waterfront Cities

A waterfront city is situated in a bay or on open water, and derives its identity largely from its waterfront. A large

number of metropolises satisfies this definition: Rio de Janeiro, Vancouver, Barcelona, Alexandria, Cape Town and Sydney are just a few examples. Their spatial structure follows a similar pattern. The centre of the city has developed historically on the water, in some cases around a small harbour, and the central districts and the highest property prices are still to be found on the waterfront. In many situations, the harbours have been moved to more spacious locations outside the city, which created space in the centre to construct boulevards, parks and other urban design elements that emphasize the relationship with the water.

There are also waterfront cities that are admittedly located on open water, but where you are hardly aware of that fact in the city centre. That is true of cities such as Mumbai, Tokyo and Buenos Aires. The Argentinean capital lies on the Río de la Plata. This forms the estuary of two other rivers, the Paraná and the Uruguay, on their way to the Atlantic Ocean. The estuary is a total of 290 km long. The water is 48 km wide where the two rivers come together; at the ocean it is 220 km. That makes the Río de la Plata

Aerial view of Rotterdam, the Netherlands, which houses the largest port in Europe. Located on the banks of the New Maas, a tributary of the Rhine and Maas Rivers, it acted as the world's largest port until Shanghai took the crown in 2004.

the largest estuary on earth, but in Buenos Aires it is not noticeable at all. A series of artificial islands in front of the city, originally located directly on the water, blocks the city's view over the water. The islands were created in the 1970s by dumping the rubble in the river from demolished buildings off Costanera Sud, pulled down to make room for the construction of motorways throughout the city. A park has now been built on the landfill. There is a formidable challenge here for Buenos Aires, and many other cities, in relation to urban design. After all, waterfront cities such as Vancouver and Sydney have demonstrated that a lively well-designed waterfront can be an important contribution to the attractiveness and therefore the economy of the city. Flexible, floating expansions can provide the functions required to turn the waterfront into a magnet for visitors.

River Cities

River cities are located on a river and owe their origins to the river. Most of the metropolises that are not waterfront cities lie on a river. Here, too, there are plenty of examples: London, Paris, Cairo, Cincinnati, Philadelphia, Seoul, Bangkok, Ho Chi Minh City, Guangzhou and Nanjing are just a few. In many American and Asian cities, the river is admittedly an important spatial element, but is cut off from city life by paved quays and motorways along the banks. As a result, the water there can only be experienced from inside a car. This is a missed opportunity in many cases.

The Korean capital Seoul, for example, is surrounded by mountains and lies on the Han: The Han is not the only river in Seoul. The Cheonggyecheon River also flows right through the city. Fifty years ago, it was a wide but shallow stream that

divided the city in two: the rich north side and the poor south side. It was once the place where clothes were washed and children played, but when the city grew from a semi-rural living area into a gigantic, smog-filled mega city, the Cheonggyecheon was reduced to an open sewer. The quays were paved over and the river bed was rebuilt as a road to cater to the increasing traffic, with a raised six-lane motorway on columns.

However, in 2002 the mayor of Seoul at that time, Lee Myung Bak, decided to restore the river to its former glory by demolishing the raised motorway and building an 8-km-long, 800-m-wide park where the river once flowed. The park and the river are now the centre of recreation and entertainment in the densely-built capital. Lee Myung Bak went on to become the President of Korea.

Another example of a river city is Bangkok. In the past, the river played a much more important role in city life than is the case today. Up until the mid-nineteenth century, the Thai capital on the Chao Phraya River was a water-rich city, with the majority of its inhabitants living on or beside a canal. Up until 1971, the city consisted of two separate parts – Krung Thep, the Thai name for

The Cheonggyecheon River redevelopment was an urban renewal project in Seoul, South Korea, focussed on reintroducing nature into the downtown district.

Nicknamed 'the Venice of the east', Bangkok used to house a large variety of khlongs (canals). Although originally used for travel, floating markets and sewage, many of these khlongs have disappeared, being converted into paved roads. On the outskirts of town, however, they can still be found, with houses scattered along their shores.

The Damnoen Saduak district, in the Ratchaburi province of Thailand, is home to a famous floating market and tourist attraction, open every morning, showing the historic importance of the river as a means of commerce.

Bangkok, on the east bank of the Chao Phraya River and Thon Buri on the west bank – connected by a large number of bridges. Many canals (khlongs) provided drainage of the marshy area around the river and made not only building possible but also a finely-branched infrastructure for the transport of people and goods, which mostly took place by boat. Trade was also mainly carried out on the water. These days, the daily floating market draws hordes of tourists in the vicinity of Wat Sai, but originally there were various similar markets in the city, and on top of that hundreds of tradesmen selling door-to-door from their boats.

The large-scale city expansions in the twentieth century and the introduction of the car drastically altered the role of the traditional waterways in Bangkok. The number of inhabitants grew from 600,000 in 1900 to more than eight million now. The number of cars grew in line with the population, so that soon there was a shortage of roads. In the second half of the twentieth century, this problem was first of all tackled by filling in virtually all the smaller canals and some of the larger ones. This was not just a major step backwards in aesthetic terms. The canal system had also functioned as drainage for the boggy delta, which led increasingly to flooding in the low-lying parts of the city during the twentieth century. Bangkok pumps its drinking water mainly from deep wells; as a result, the ground is becoming lower in many places. That not only worsens the effects of flooding, it also leads to contaminated water.

The process of urbanization occurred fastest in the centre of the city on the east bank of the Chao Phraya River. The khlongs on the Bangkok side of the city have almost all disappeared. The few khlongs still to be found on the east side of the city, in Thon Buri, represent only a shadow of Bangkok's watery past. There are still many boats on the Chao Phraya itself, but the paved quays offer very little space for urban life beside the water.

In these types of densely-built cities, where wide rivers provide the space missing on land, and where motorways cut the water off from the city, floating urban expansions on the water could not only accommodate new functions but also improve the quality of life by once again making the river an integral part of the city.

London, another river city, has a completely different problem: flood zones. The Thames, which flows through the city, is a tidal river and therefore has many fluctuations in level. After the catastrophic flooding in 1953, the Thames Barrier was built: a flood barrier in the river at Woolwich, a district in the east of the city. However, the city had to expand beyond the flood barrier and, as a result, there are areas that are regularly flooded by water from the Thames.

The Thames Gateway, as the 60-km-long region between the London Docklands and the Thames Estuary is known, is the largest regeneration area in the Great Britain at the moment. This neglected area houses around 1.6 million people. The British government invests enormous sums of money to combat poor-quality public transport, inadequate services, high unemployment and substandard housing. Large-scale building plans, including those for the Olympic Games in 2012, form an important part of the project.

However, there is also a lot of opposition. The Thames Gateway project contains plans to lay dry the North Kent Marshes, considered an 'environmentally sensitive area' by the government, and start building. The area is, however, of great ecological importance. The marshes are regularly flooded and that gives them not just a unique ecosystem, but also serves as natural water storage that protects the city of London from flooding. Of course, new artificial water storage areas could be created at a high cost, but the most clever solution lies much closer to home: floating residential neighbourhoods, where the buildings move in rhythm with the tidal fluctuations, could not only be created without causing any scars and in so doing maintain the unique marshes, but could also make the creation of artificial water storage unnecessary.

Canal Cities

In canal cities, the city canals constitute the most important structuring element. The canals are necessary to drain the land; canal cities are generally situated in wet regions. In addition, the canals originally accommodated a substantial part of the infrastructure: they served as the main thoroughfares for the transport of people and goods and a weekly flush ensured

HUMAN INTERFERENCE
REGULARLY
LEADS TO PROBLEMS
WITH WATER

that the city remained clean. Amsterdam, Bruges and St Petersburg are a few examples, with Amsterdam as the prototype of a structured, rationally built canal city.

Amsterdam originally lay in a boggy marsh delta that was drained by means of an expansive system of small dikes and ditches. A dam was built in the Amstel River around 1270. In the late Middle Ages, the centre of Amsterdam came into being on both sides of the canalized and dammed stretch of the Amstel.

The famous canals that now adorn every picture postcard of the city were dug in the seventeenth century, when the city experienced the peak of its wealth and power.

The city owed a large part of its prosperity to its location on the water. The ships of the Dutch East India Company and the Dutch West India Company set sail from Amsterdam on their trade journeys to the farthest corners of the globe, and the battle fleet that fought against Spain and England also left from here. Within the city, too, a great deal of the transport took place over water. The current city councillors have not forgotten the past; in the search for alternatives to the air pollution caused by road traffic and increasingly blocked streets, the canals are once again 'in the picture'. In February 2010, the city administration accepted the 'Smart and Clean Urban Distribution Amsterdam' plan that provides for the stocking of shops over water; it should lead to a significant decrease in the number of lorries in the city.[17]

Archipelago Cities

Archipelago cities are built on several, in some cases artificial islands, surrounded by water. These cities are often located in a lagoon: a sort of lake that has come into existence between a beach and a promontory or sandspit, usually with an open connection to the sea. But archipelago cities can also be found in a delta: a system of river branches before they flow out into the sea or a large lake. On the map a system like this is shaped like a triangle, which explains the name delta (the Greek letter Δ). In Scandinavia, archipelago cities are often located close to fiords: Stockholm and Helsinki, for instance.

A number of cities that would now be classified as waterfront cities used to be archipelago cities. A good example of this is Mumbai. This city once consisted of an archipelago of seven small islands, which the British transformed into a large peninsula called Salsette from 1782 onwards, with the help of large-scale civil engineering works. This project, known as Hornby Vellard, was completed in 1845 and resulted in 438 km² of extra land surface.

The model of an archipelago city is of course Venice. This city owed its wealth and power in the fifteenth century in particular to its position on the water. Venice was an important sea power and was able to completely control trade with the Levant, due to its location. Transport of both people and goods took place mainly over water; boats had the same function as cars in a modern city. Transport of people was carried out originally in gondolas, but these are now used only by tourists

Maps showing Mumbai (Bombay) originally as an archipelago and then once it was transformed by the British in 1845. Today the city is the second largest in population, with just under 14 million inhabitants, being only slightly behind Shanghai.

and for special occasions. These days, Venice's own inhabitants travel mainly by motorized water buses: the Vaporetti.

Due to its position in the Laguna Veneta, Venice often has to contend with flooding from the Adriatic Sea, particularly between November and February. Due to the marshy ground, the buildings in Venice are built on piles, just like in Amsterdam. In November 1966, Venice was afflicted by unprecedented flooding, which caused a great deal of damage to the countless art treasures. Human interference regularly leads to problematic situations as well. In the twentieth century, pumping away the groundwater under the city for the chemical industry led to considerable subsidence and, as a result, the city was in danger of sinking away. For this reason, it was forbidden in the 1960s. In addition, the water level rose. Compared to 100 years earlier, the average water level in 2003 had risen by 24 cm. In order to prevent further flooding, work was started in 2003 on the building of a storm surge to close off the lagoon at high tide.

Another example of an archipelago city is Hong Kong; one of the most built-up cities in the world. Hong Kong

consists of the island with the same
name to the east of the Zhujiang River,
the peninsula of Kowloon and the New
Territories. The New Territories is
the area to the north of Kowloon that
borders on mainland China. It consists
of more than 200 islands, the majority
of which are uninhabited. So water in
Hong Kong is never far away.

View looking north from
Hong Kong Island with
the city's tall skyscrapers
looming over the harbour.
The Kowloon Peninsula can
be seen across the water
with the Hong Kong cultural
centre, Salisbury Garden
and Avenue of the Stars
branching into the harbour.

No more building takes place
on any of the islands. The built-up areas are completely full
and the undeveloped islands cannot be built on due to the
mountains. In the past there has been a certain amount of land
reclamation but that has been stopped now, because it had too
great an effect on the quality of the water and the cityscape.
The city administration is now investigating how to accommodate parts of the infrastructure on water. However, buoyancy
techniques are not being utilized at all yet. The same axiom
holds true for Hong Kong: the city can be made more pleasant
to live in by using the water.

Island Cities

Island cities are built on a single, fully built-up island. Just like
archipelago cities, they are mostly found in lagoons and deltas.
Examples are Flores, a city in Lake Peten Itza in Guatemala,
and Mexcaltitan in the Nayarit coastal marshes in Mexico.
The Mexican capital was once an island city called Tenochtitlan. The settlement consisted of a 12-15-km^2 island in the
Texcoco lake in the Basin of Mexico. After the Spaniards had
definitely conquered Tenochtitlan in 1521 and renamed it

Reproduction of the map
attached to the convention
between Great Britain and
China signed in Peking on 9
June 1898.

Mexico City, they filled in the many canals dug by the Aztecs to make way for
roads, and little by little they drained
large areas of the lake. These days,
almost the entire Basin of Mexico has
been filled in, which has paradoxically
enough led to considerable problems in
urban water management.

A prime example of an island
city still in existence is Malé, the capital
of the Maldives. This city with its more
than 100,000 inhabitants covers the

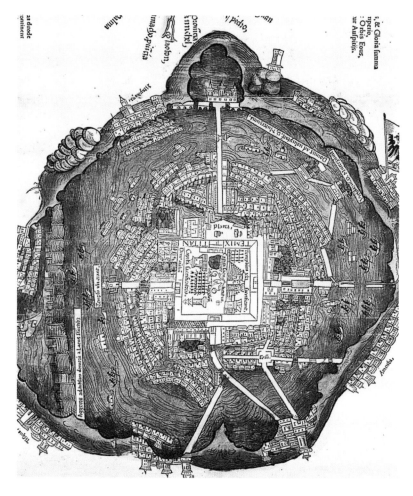

Map showing the ancient Aztec island city of Teno-chtitlan, located on Lake Texcoco. Upon defeating the Aztecs in 1521, the Spaniards built what is now present-day Mexico City upon the Ruins of the Aztec city, draining much of the lake in the process.

entire island of Malé, part of the Kaafu Atoll. The island measures a mere 1 x 1.7 km and is completely built-up. The Maldives themselves are an island group consisting of 1190 coral islands grouped into 26 atolls in the Indian Ocean, southwest of India. The islands are spread out over a surface area of approximately 90,000 km², but the total land surface is only around 298 km². The largest island is 5 km² in size;

The island town of Mexcalti-tlan, Nayarit, Mexico.

there are only nine larger than 2 km². Two hundred islands are inhabited and another 88 are tourist resorts.

The Maldives have a big problem. Of the islands, 80 per cent are less than 60 cm above water level. That makes 1,190 islands spread over 26 atolls. On 26 December 2004, the islands were almost completely flooded by a tsunami caused by an earthquake

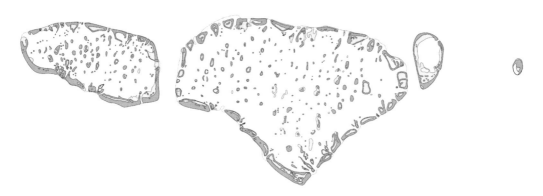

in the Indian Ocean. Furthermore, scientists are taking into account a possible rise in sea level of almost 1 m. More than 300,000 people live on the Maldives and billions are earned with tourism. President Mohammed Nasheed said in early 2009: we are going to buy land in Sri Lanka and we are going to move the entire Maldives. But there is an alternative. It is now technologically feasible to create islands that look exactly the same as the Maldives, with the same vegetation, beaches and waves, without having a negative effect on the coral. In fact: technologically, it is possible to convert a great number of those tourist attractions into hybrid systems, in a programme lasting around 50 years. Perhaps this sounds drastic, but it is a much less radical solution than relocating an entire country.

The Republic of Maldives is a cluster of 26 separate atolls in the Indian Ocean, which together form the smallest country in Asia, both in regard to population and area.

FROM WATER CITIES
TO HYDROCITIES

Water cities have been around just as long as there have been cities. Hydrocities are the cities of the future. What is the difference between the two? A water city is a city located on the water, but built on land. A hydrocity is a city structure where both land and water are the carriers of urban functions, infrastructure and identity. A hydrocity is not an ideal city structure on water, but the improved version of an existing city on the water, where the boundary between wet and dry is no longer relevant. As a consequence, there is no generic blueprint for a hydrocity. The hydrocity is not the result of a single, large-scale, all-embracing plan, which can be built in one fell swoop, but can be realized in small steps, depending on demand, locally available technology and public support. The hydrocity is an upgrade, a 2.0 version of each of the six existing city configurations already mentioned, where water is used for conservation, improvement or density. Here are a few examples.

Conservation

As described earlier, Venice has two problems: the sea level is rising and the city is sinking. In the course of a century, Venice has lost around 24 cm in relation to the water. Perhaps that does not sound like very much, but those 24 cm are threatening the continued undamaged existence of the city to a significant degree.

However, not just the problems caused by rising sea levels and subsidence need to be solved to preserve the city for eternity. Venice is actually an impossible city. The buildings have their feet in salt water and that has such enormous consequences for the foundations and the load-bearing walls that the buildings have to be continuously maintained. The salt water is absorbed into the walls, pushes away the stucco and breaks off the bricks. Venice is an artificial city: the non-stop maintenance with its resulting exorbitant costs is the only thing keeping up the historical buildings.

If Venice were a hydro-archipelago city, all its problems would be solved at a single stroke. In the hydro-archipelago city Venice, all the existing foundation piles would be replaced with floating foundations. It would be an unbelievably expensive operation, but one which would maintain its worth for centuries and could therefore be written off over many hundreds of years.

The procedure is relatively simple. First of all, sheet piling would be driven in round an individual building or block of buildings. The building pit would then be pumped dry and the space between the foundation piles dug out. Subsequently, formwork would be installed for new foundations made of concrete and polystyrene foam or another buoyant construction. The total weight of the building (dynamic and static) and the centre of gravity would determine the size of the new floating foundations. When the foundations are ready, the building pit would be partly filled in with water up to the

point where the new foundations experience sufficient upwards thrust to ensure that the pressure on the piles is virtually non-existent. After this, the old pile foundations sticking through the new foundations would be levelled off and the building would float. The floating building would be connected to the existing utilities by means of flexible pipes.

Not only buildings but also city squares could be replaced by buoyant versions. In optical terms, the result would not look any different than the existing city.

Malé is the capital city of the Republic of Maldives. Located at the southern edge of the North Malé Atoll, which itself is part of the Kaafu Atoll, the central island of the city is almost completely developed through human urbanization.

Improvement

As already said, hydrocities are upgrades of the existing city, where the use of water gives new urban qualities to the city. Improving the living climate can cause a water city to turn into a hydrocity. What about Seoul, for instance? Mayor Lee Myung Bak restored the Cheonggyecheon River to its former glory, but hydro-river city Seoul goes one step further.

The river Han is an ideal open building site in the city centre, due to its 1-km width. That provides sufficient room to improve the existing city. Floating parks for golf and recreation, buoyant beaches to restore the relationship between the city and the water and floating parking areas to free up the more expensive land for building. The possibilities are endless. Hydro-river city Seoul could grow over the river region by 30 per cent, for example. The flow of the river would hardly be influenced by the floating urban design and river traffic would have more than enough space in the 70 m of the 1000 m available to provide a solution to road congestion in the city centre. Once floating living and working functions appear on the water, it is a natural step to private and public transport on the river. As a result, the connections between the banks of the river are no longer exclusively dependent on fixed elements such as bridges and the underground system.

Hydro-river cities provide space for both new urban developments and the river itself. Rivers need space, otherwise disasters can occur. In the past, rivers could all become larger or smaller, because there were outlet areas. But due to the pressure of building, many rivers in cities were canalized at a given moment. The same happened in many Asian and American cities: high concrete edges were constructed to ensure that the buildings behind could remain dry. But in the meantime, the contact between land and water was completely severed. For a tidal river, the solution could be, for example, a park that bridges the height difference between land and water. The problem, however, is that the park gets flooded at high tide. By introducing floating parks, the flow of the river can be preserved; the parks will never get flooded because they rise and fall with the rhythm of the water.

Density

There is fierce global competition raging between the large port cities. Volume is everything and ships are becoming increasingly efficient because they keep getting bigger. Ports need space for container transhipment; old harbour cities cannot provide that space. The result is a shift of harbour activities from small-scale docks close to the centre towards large open port locations near open water.

For a long time, Rotterdam was the world's largest port, but it has now been outstripped by Chinese harbours. Although the Dutch port city has significantly increased its possibilities for growth by adding the Second Maas Area, it has lost its pole position due to the constantly increasing demand for cheap transhipment space by large ocean-going ships. At the same time, the growing demand has stripped the docks in the centre of old harbour cities of their port activities. The inner-city harbours are too small and too expensive for large ships. Hydro-port city Rotterdam would use the freed-up space for housing. The city would become denser, starting from the former inner city docks. On land, that has already happened, for example on the Kop van Zuid. This former harbour island with warehouses is now one of the most expensive residential areas in Rotterdam. The same development would take place in hydro-port city Rotterdam, but this time on the water, where living and working functions would be wrapped around the edges of the harbour like a ribbon. These developments could make use of the infrastructure on land; roads and utilities are directly available for the floating functions. Density can be further increased if buoyant high-rise is developed. Floating high-rises on floating boulevards at the edge of the port would transform the appearance of Rotterdam from the water. Rotterdam hydro-port city is a hybrid city, where both land and water provide space to increase density.

IN A HYDROCITY, THE BOUNDARY BETWEEN WET AND DRY IS NO LONGER RELEVANT

Urban Transport over Water

One of the characteristics of the hydrocity is that water does not only serve as a building location, but that it also plays an important role in the infrastructure. All over the world, urban transport is principally dependent on the car. For the majority of metropolises, motorized transport is the driving force behind urban mobility and logistics. Cities such as London, Tokyo and New York admittedly have the underground, and it would be hard to imagine those cities without it, but the car has dominated urban infrastructure for decades due to its ease, speed and low costs; it has pushed every other form of mobility out of the market, particularly in the area of public transport. Take the USA, for example. Around 1900 there were still

40,000 km of electric streetcar tracks; by 1930 the entire system had virtually disappeared. The tracks were bought up by car manufacturers and subsequently shut down. In their place came cars and buses, many of them produced by Yellow Coach and used by bus services such as Greyhound. The owner of these companies was – not surprisingly – also a car manufacturer: General Motors. For decades, the powerful car industry lobby managed to achieve a great deal in American politics, but this history has turned against the company these days, now that GM (and its consorts) is also accused of doing too little in recent years to develop clean engines.

Venice is one of the few famous world cities where water is the most important form of transport. Only in one small part of the city are there any cars at all. Everything travels by water: rubbish collection, deliveries and transport of goods, public and private transport. The water motorway is a wonderful sight: large poles in the water mark the route from Venice to the airport and speedboats are allowed to open their throttles.

Changes relating to mobility in the city happen slowly, but just like the USA in the second half of the twentieth

Based on a series of studies completed by the Latrobe Team, a multidisciplinary group with affiliations to Princeton University, Rising Currents: Projects for New York's Waterfront is a response to economical and infrastructural issues that could drastically affect the future of the New York/New Jersey region. Feeling that traditional drainage systems and storm-surge barriers were too ineffective and expensive to feasibly protect the area, the team emphasized the need to explore alternative 'soft infrastructures'. A master plan for the Upper Bay was created that explored the use of designed wetlands, artificial islands and reefs created with old subway cars, as a means to more ecologically battle the effects of global warming and the city's infrastructural dilemmas. This plan became the point of departure for the five design teams participating in the MOMA exhibition that opened March 2010. Each of the five teams were given a zone within the Upper Bay to further explore the possibilities of these proposed soft infrastructures.

century, when the supremacy of the car was achieved by deliberate political and economic choices, it is possible to redefine city transport now. Venice's water transport can serve as an excellent example.

Hydrocity New York, a 75-m-Deep Polder in the Ocean

Finally, a city that forms an exception in all the categories described earlier: New York. The Big Apple is an island city (if you only consider Manhattan – which is actually a peninsula), an archipelago city (if you count Staten Island, Governors Island and Long Island, for instance) and a river city (if you regard the Hudson as the life line of the city). It is clear that water is important to New York; people are also beginning to realize that water could be a potential threat, as was shown in the exhibition 'Rising Currents: Projects for New York's Waterfront',

Zone 0: Lower Manhattan (ARO and dlandstudio) Using both soft and hard infrastructures, the project introduces new wetlands along Lower Manhattan's coast and integrates new 'natural' streetscapes that absorb, rather than relocate, runoff.

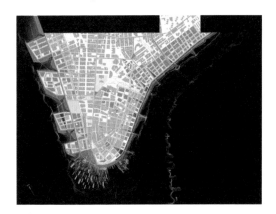

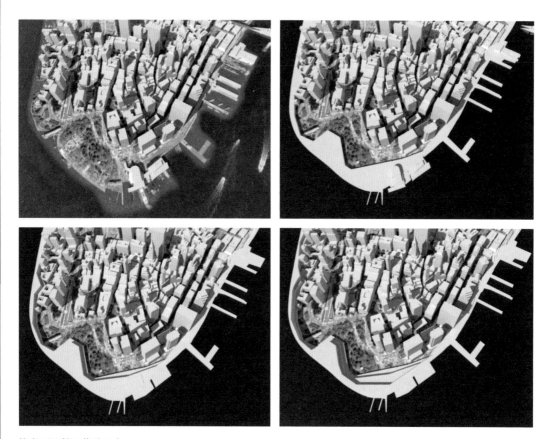

Hydrocity New York, a design for Manhattan to deal with the situation of the sea level rising 3.75 m per decade for two centuries – a total of 75 m in 200 years. An enormous flood barrier protects the lower part of the island.

held from March to October 2010 in the Museum of Modern Art in New York. Five architects (LTL Architects, Matthew Baird Architects, nARCHITECTS, SCAPE and ARO) made proposals for the way New York should deal with rising sea levels.

National Geographic painted a much grimmer picture than was shown at the exhibition, and asked Waterstudio to make a design for New York to deal with the situation of the sea level rising 3.75 m per decade for two centuries – a total of 75 m in 200 years.

The first question raised by such an enormous rise is, of course, whether a city could and should be preserved in a situation like this. Through urbanization and globalization, the world is changing from a group of countries with cities into a group of metropolises that are more important to the world economy than the countries to which they belong. This means that the metropolises transcend the nation states as an economic and geopolitical factor. These megacities have their own specific identity. And that identity makes preservation worthwhile, even if the cost of preservation is higher than the economic product of those cities.

New York lies in the heart of the Mega Region New York-Boston-Washington, to pull out a term coined by sociologist and urbanist Richard Florida. In turn, Manhattan is the soul of New York. By an extreme rise in the level of the sea, the suburbs of New York would gradually be adapted during the 3.75 m rise per decade, by replacing the existing buildings bit by bit with floating city components, but for Manhattan that is not only impossible but also undesirable. On the other hand, Manhattan is building an enormous flood barrier round the island. This megastructure – a sort of superlative version of the Hoover Dam – is kept out of sight by building skyscrapers up against it, which simultaneously should make the whole operation financially feasible. On the water side of the wall, 75 m above the streets of Manhattan, there are floating piers on a quay, called New Wall Street. These piers, with dock facilities and entertainment functions, ensure that the city retains the same relationship with the water that it has now. After all, the river rises with the sea.

The wall does not need to be constructed 75 m high in one go; it can grow gradually in the course of 200 years.

Once the process is complete, Manhattan will be a polder in the ocean; land kept artificially dry and surrounded by city applications for housing, workspace, recreation, agriculture and sustainable floating power plants. Seen from the air, the city will not look much different from now, but in reality it will have become an enormous bathtub with a buoyant, dynamic city around it. And if the sea level really does rise by 75 m, this scenario will not just be reserved for New York. Amsterdam, London, Rome and all those other well-loved metropolises on the water can be preserved in the same way. Anywhere the city constitutes an important part of the identity of a people, that city will be worth preserving.

The hydrocity is a step in the evolution of the water city. The way and the degree to which a water city transforms

ONCE THE MEGASTRUC- TURE IS COMPLETE, MANHATTAN WILL BE A POLDER IN THE OCEAN

into a hydrocity depends on the necessity for that city to adapt to change. The hydrocity is a chameleon. If the sea level really does rise by metres, the hydrocity will naturally be profiled more extremely than if the climate change does not persist. But even without a rising sea level, it is clear that the hydrocity represents huge potential for the growth of water cities worldwide.

STATIC

POLDER

S BECOM

IE DYNA

MIC

Large parts of the Netherlands are under sea level.
The Ijsselmeer (left) is
significantly higher than the
Uitdammer Die (right) and
the surrounding polders,
just north of Amsterdam.

Chapter 5

HOLLAND 2.0 DEPOLDERIZED

The Netherlands is known throughout the world for its struggle with water. The icon of this struggle is the polder system, an artificial scheme of reclaimed land enclosed by dikes. However, the Dutch landscape has not always been man-made. A thousand years ago, the west of what is now called the Netherlands was a boggy marsh delta. The Rhine, Waal and Meuse rivers flowed out of inland Europe into the North Sea at that point. The pieces of land between the broad river mouths were marshy, and the people who settled in these unlikely surroundings were smart enough to build their dwellings on the scarce pieces of dry land that were above the water level at that time. That is why the historical centres of many old cities, including Amsterdam, are just above sea level, while the newer expansion districts are often situated much lower.

Beeldenstorm (Destruction of images) in a Church, 1630, painted by Dirck van Delen (Heusden, ca. 1604-1605 – Arnemuiden, 1671), Rijksmuseum Amsterdam.

Before long the dry areas had all been used and measures had to be taken to make the rest of the country habitable. A great deal of creativity was unleashed in the process. Anyone who knows a little about the history of the Netherlands knows that the people who settled here had a hard time of it. The Low Lands were regularly attacked by other European powers. There were problems with the Roman Catholic Church. There was a shortage of natural commodities. Water and wind formed a constant threat to the living environment. But with every new challenge, the 'Hollanders' were prepared to adapt and turn the drawbacks to their advantage. They stormed the Roman Catholic churches to pull down the statues of the saints, and they gave the power of the nobility to the people. They began trading worldwide with the Dutch East India Company, the first multinational on earth. They turned water into land and used mills to obtain energy from the wind. That is how the Dutch landscape came into being; it was fought for with human lives and made with human hands, something everyone takes for granted these days.

At the same time, everyone knows that that idyllic Dutch landscape hardly exists any more. In order to prevent the land ending up under water, it has gradually been transformed into one great masterpiece of civil engineering. In that respect, the Netherlands is fake. In other words, the landscape is artificial. These days, the work is carried out by electric pumping stations. They do not operate on wind energy and are therefore more reliable, but they are also a good deal less environmentally friendly than windmills. In addition, they

The Dutch landscape is a succession of rectilinear pieces of infrastructure that have completely obscured the underlying original polder landscape. Aerial photo of the A4 motorway at Leiderdorp and Nieuw-Vennep.

are a lot less visible. As a result, Dutch people are beginning to forget that they live in an artificial landscape. And that is not the only reason. The pristine system of polders, dikes and canals is like an abstract painting to which an increasing number of stripes and spots have been added. Motorways, aqueducts, tunnels, bridges, power pylons, new city plans and industrial estates

The highest point in the
Netherlands is situated on
the Vaalserberg in Limburg
and lies 322.4 m above
NAP (Normal Amsterdam
Water Level). However, by
far the largest part of the
country is no more than 6 m
high. The lowest point is in
Nieuwerkerk aan den IJssel,
6.76 m under NAP. All the
blue and turquoise areas are
under sea level.

Legend in metres

■	-12 › -7	■	8 › 9
■	-7 › -6	■	9 › 10
■	-6 › -5	■	10 › 12
■	-5 › -4	■	12 › 14
■	-4 › -3		14 › 16
■	-3 › -2,5		16 › 18
■	-2,5 › -2		18 › 20
■	-2 › -1,5	■	20 › 25
■	-1,5 › -1	■	25 › 30
■	-1 › -0,5	■	30 › 35
■	-0,5 › 0	■	35 › 40
■	0 › 0,5	■	40 › 45
■	0,5 › 1	■	45 › 50
■	1 › 1,5	■	50 › 60
■	1,5 › 2	■	60 › 70
■	2 › 2,5	■	70 › 80
■	2,5 › 3	■	80 › 90
■	3 › 3,5	■	90 › 100
■	3,5 › 4	■	100 › 125
■	4 › 4,5	■	125 › 150
■	4,5 › 5	■	150 › 175
■	5 › 6	■	175 › 200
■	6 › 7	■	200 › 250
■	7 › 8	■	250 › 300
		■	300 › 350

create an autonomous infrastructure that is becoming more and more dense, making the polders in the layer underneath increasingly invisible. All these facilities ensure that people can move around quickly and that they can live and work, but they have completely obscured the view of the original landscape.

As a result, visitors to the Netherlands who are professionally interested in water management are often disappointed if they ask a random passer-by at a random spot for information about the landscape. Are we above or below sea level here? Which dikes protect this area? How many polders are there in the Netherlands? Most inhabitants will have no idea what the answers are to these questions. The average Dutch person does know in abstract terms that 20 per cent of his country lies below sea level and that more than 30 per cent belongs to the category 'potential flooding region', under influence of factors such as the tides. The average water level at high tide is around 0.5 to 2.5 m higher than the Normaal Amsterdams Peil – the Normal Amsterdam Level; a NAP height of 0 m is approximately equivalent to the average between low and high tide in the North Sea. During spring tide, high tide is even higher. Furthermore, the tides create upward pressure in the rivers. As a result, if there were no dikes, approximately one third of the country would be under water. The Randstad, the most densely populated and economically important region in the west of the Netherlands would become almost completely inhabitable.

Up to this point, most Dutch people know the situation. But understanding the consequences for their own direct living environment is something most people haven't got a clue about. It is not the fault of a shortage of general information services: by simply entering their postcode on the website Actueel Hoogtebestand Nederland, for example, every resident can easily find out the height of his street in

IF THERE WERE NO DIKES, ONE THIRD OF THE NETHERLANDS WOULD BE UNDER WATER

relation to sea level. In addition, since March 2005, 23 signs have decorated the Dutch landscape and show the 'real coastline' of the Netherlands: at the points where motorways cross the NAP, special markings have been installed in the form of information panels. There are countless other initiatives to increase the awareness of Dutch residents about their living environment. Nonetheless, most people have no idea about the sort of landscape they live in.[18]

Part of the problem is the paternalistic system in place in the Netherlands. The government has been saying for years: go to sleep, everything is fine. The dikes are safe. But the government doesn't know exactly what 'safe' is. 'We have reduced the chance of flooding from 1:4,000 to 1:10,000,' was written in an official report, for example. But what does that mean? What can you do with this information as a resident of the country? If you buy a house, you should be able to find out how high the risk of flooding is. What is the dike made of? How is it maintained? If the water rises, how high will it come? How fast? And what should I do? Should I get myself to higher ground or drive away? What would happen to my house if there were 60 cm of water in it? What would happen afterwards? Who will pay for the damage? The government does not have to pay and neither do the insurance companies. Floods are natural disasters and if you buy a house in a low-lying area, it's too bad if it's flooded.

For example, an uninsured incident took place on 26 August 2003 in Wilnis in Utrecht: in the middle of the night, a dike suddenly collapsed, causing great panic and dozens of houses full of water for days on end. The dike was apparently weakened by the persistent drought. The Netherlands has around 5,000 km of this sort of vulnerable little peat dikes, clay dikes and sea dikes. All built of natural materials. Not until after the disaster in Wilnis did Delft University of Technology develop a piece of equipment that can be used to carry out geological investigation into how strong such a dike really is.

A house in a low polder in the densely populated west of the Netherlands is more expensive than a lovely dry house in the sparsely populated south. That is because the risk of

On 26 August 2003, the water in the Ringvaart (Ring Canal) near the village of Wilnis in the province of Utrecht smashed a 60-m hole in the Ring Dike. As a result, water flowed into the village streets, and 2,000 people were evacuated from the affected neighbourhood. The cause turned out to be poor maintenance in combination with the effects of drought. Just like many other dikes in the Netherlands, this one consisted mainly of peat, which absorbs water. However, persistent dry weather had made the dike so light that it began to shift.

flooding is not included in the price. In the Netherlands, thousands of people live behind dikes that are not entirely safe. And still many house buyers are only interested in whether they like the building and if the location is good. But the technology used in the foundations and safety aspects are not considered. And so houses are built almost 7 m below sea level in a location such as the Zuidplas Polder near Gouda, without any possibility of insuring against the risk of flooding. There the District Water Boards pump like crazy and the government says: it is safe, but we give no guarantees.

Things could be different. A country such as Japan also has to deal with natural dangers. They not only have the risk of flash floods from rivers, because large parts of the country are paved over, but earthquakes and typhoons are also frequent phenomena. The residents are exposed to many sorts of danger and the government does not say: you really are safe. So the Japanese are used to a government that gives information. If you know there is a risk of flooding, you don't go and sit in the underground. If you are in an area where water comes in every so often, you don't build there. This sort of culture is unknown in the Netherlands.

The paternalistic system really is completely outdated. General knowledge about the landscape and rising water used to be widely known, when fluctuating water levels were part of daily reality. Taking partial responsibility by acquiring a general level of knowledge about the water management system would not be a bad thing in the Netherlands these days, too.

What Is a Polder?

The Netherlands has approximately 3,500 polders: areas that are situated lower than the surrounding water and are protected by water barriers, usually in the form of dikes. The water level in a polder is artificially regulated by a polder mill or a pumping station. A polder (sometimes also known as a dike-ring area) is an official water unit; it has no connection with external water other than via man-made works. There are polders in different types and sizes. The three most important forms are reclaimed land, diked-in land and reclamation development. Reclaimed land is land reclaimed from open water, for instance a lake or pond that has been drained. Diked-in land is when polders are created in tidal areas along the coast or a river. Such areas already fell dry periodically, and due to

diking-in they remain definitely dry and can be cultivated. On the coast these areas are usually mud flats, along rivers they are former forelands. Finally, reclamation development is a cultivated piece of waste ground, for instance former marsh, peat, heath or dune ground. It is not necessarily a polder; that name is used only if the area has to be continuously drained.

Inpoldering is not a one-off operation, where after constructing the dikes you can say: and that was that. It is a never-ending task. Every one of the 3,500 polders has to be continuously drained to keep it dry: 24 hours a day, seven days a week, all year long. In the past this task was carried out by windmills. Patiently, step by step, they pumped water from the lowest-lying site a few centimetres higher to the next site. The next windmill did the same again, until the water was at the level of the nearest natural water and could be drained away. It led to an ingenious, many-branched system of countless level planes: +10 cm NAP, -15 cm NAP, +40 cm NAP. For many Dutch people, the beautiful landscape that resulted from this unprecedented piece of engineering mastery expresses the essence of their national character: endlessly flat land as far as the eye can see, broken here and there by a church steeple or a windmill. It has nothing to do with nature. The landscape is for the most part man-made.

Marken, a small village near Amsterdam in the Netherlands. The houses are packed together in an exposed situation on a small piece of high dry land. On the right, the IJsselmeer, on the left the much lower-lying polder.

Take the Haarlemmermeer Polder, for instance. The Haarlemmermeer was once the largest lake in Holland and was located between the historical cities of Amsterdam, Haarlem and Leiden. It consisted originally of three separate peaty lakes, which merged into the Haarlemmermeer round 1500 after heavy storms; it has a surface area of almost 170 km². The lake continued to grow considerably in the centuries afterwards. The water swallowed up a number of villages, including Nieuwerkerk, Rijk and Vijfhuizen. When the water finally reached the gates of Leiden and Amsterdam, King Willem I decided in 1837 that the lake should be drained. In 1852, the task was complete. The Ringvaart (Ring Canal), more than 60 km long, enclosed 185 km² of pristine new land.

These days, the Haarlemmermeer is the economic powerhouse of the Amsterdam region. Schiphol Airport is the fourth largest airport in Europe, with approximately 50 million passengers per year. An enormous number of companies are established around Schiphol, where thousands of people work every day. Hoofddorp, Nieuw-

(Top)
The Haarlemmermeer before land reclamation. The dotted lines with dates represent the size of the lake as time passed. It shows how the Haarlemmermeer grew from a series of lakes into one big inland sea. Drawn in the nineteenth century, based on the 1740 original by Melchior Bolstra.

(Bottom)
The Haarlemmermeer after land reclamation.

Vennep and the other new places in the polder provide a home to more than 140,000 people. Every day, a large number of people use the A4 motorway to travel from Amsterdam to Rotterdam. When they drive into the polder, they go under the Ringvaart. Most people find the aqueduct attractive at this spot, but they have no idea that they are going into a deep polder, that they are driving from old to new land. More than 150 years ago, people were digging channels there in the mud with their bare hands for years on end. The amount of blood, sweat and tears shed there is unimaginable. Today, hardly anyone is aware of this as they speed down the motorway from Amsterdam to Rotterdam.

The Polder as Defence Mechanism

Polders usually have an agricultural function. In the Nether-lands, however, they also had a defence function for a long time. King Willem I (there he is again; he played an important role in Dutch public works) decided in 1815 to construct another feat of civil engineering: the New Dutch Waterline. Both the New Dutch Waterline and the Defence Line of Amsterdam consisted of a system of polders that could be submerged if there were threats from outside: so-called inun-dation. The New Dutch Waterline lay as a protective garland round the cities of Holland, 85 km long and 3 to 5 km wide. A total of 46 forts and five fortified towns (including Muiden, Weesp and Naarden) were meant to protect Holland from attack. The Defence Line of Amsterdam was likewise a strip of land flooded as a defence line, situated 10 to 15 km around the centre of the city. This line was 135 km long, contained 45 forts and was constructed between 1880 and 1920. As with any water defence line, the intention was to create an inun-dated area at least several kilometres wide over the entire length, which would be flooded to a depth of 30 to 60 cm: too deep for infantry to be able to march, but too shallow for normal vessels to sail on.

 The Defence Line of Amsterdam was never used; the New Dutch Waterline was completely or partly inundated three times as a consequence of threats of war: in 1870 (Franco-Prussian War), in the period 1914-1918 (First World War) and in 1939-1940 (Second World War). Inundation had proved itself many times in the history of the Netherlands as an excellent defence tactic. The best-known example is the Siege of Leiden in 1574, during the Dutch War of Independ-ence between Spain and the Low Countries, where pierced dikes and rising water put the Spaniards besieging the city to flight. But during the Second World War, it turned out that the defence tactic had been made completely redundant by the arrival of the aeroplane. In spite of the inundated polders, the Germans occupied the Netherlands within five days.[19]

 In the same way that inundation played an important role in the country's defences for centuries, but has now been overtaken by modern war tactics, the question is whether the polder system, in its current form, is in danger of being over-taken by the facts. The current structure of the Netherlands is not the final destination. The artificial landscape requires

For a long time, the New Dutch Waterline (in light blue) did service defend-ing Holland and it replaced the Dutch Waterline, which dated from the late sev-enteenth century (in dark blue). Both lines consisted of a series of empty polders that could be inundated if war threatened. The first sketches for the New Dutch Waterline date from the end of the eighteenth century. Cornelis Krayenhoff, direc-tor of the Dutch Fortifi-cations, argued in favour of shifting the old Dutch Waterline in an easterly direction, so that Utrecht would also fall within the line. In 1815, Willem I, Prince of Orange decided to implement the plan. Besides the polders, the new line also included 46 forts and five fortified towns.

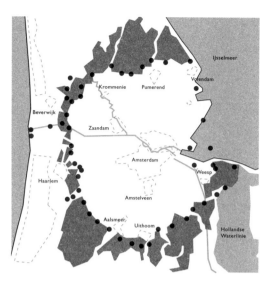

The Defence Line of Amsterdam was constructed between 1880 and 1920 and consisted of a series of low-lying polders that could be set under water in the case of hostilities. Reinforcement was provided by 45 forts, situated in locations where the waterline was crossed by dikes, roads or railway lines. The military status of the defence line was removed in 1963.

continuous maintenance and adjustment. Furthermore, every spatial intervention brings new problems.

Who Is in Charge of the Water?

The political system in the Netherlands is based on the internationally known polder model. The polder model is the name for the consultative structure between employers, employees and government authorities, aimed at reaching consensus. The concept originates from the hydrological administration system in the Netherlands. The only way to drain excess water off to open water is by continual collaboration between the users of adjacent polders. Without a good relationship with the neighbours, the intricate system of small-scale canals, dikes and pumping stations cannot function.

It will come as no surprise that in a country that owes its right of existence to the extent to which it manages to control water, the authorities involved in water levels have an important say when it comes to the decisions related to spatial structure. In the Netherlands these authorities are called District Water Boards.

Their task is to regulate water management in a particular region. The boundaries of these regions do not coincide with municipal or provincial borders, but are determined by the basins of rivers and other inland waters. The District Water Boards, of which there are 26, belong to the oldest democratic institutions in the Netherlands and hold a special place in Dutch legal history. It is their task to regulate water management in a particular region on behalf of the inhabitants. Their work is in the public interest. Every four years, Dutch people vote in the district water board elections to choose a board consisting of a Dike Reeve and Dike Board, comparable to the bench of Mayor and Aldermen in a municipality.

Dutch people are no longer aware of the importance of the District Water Boards, so these elections do not attract any interest. In 2008, the turnout was 24 per cent. However, the Water Boards represent a hugely underestimated power factor. The people who work there determine to a large degree what the Netherlands look like and what happens there. But a large part of what they do takes place behind the scenes. Many people would rather read in the newspapers about the latest disturbances in parliament than be up to date on the fortunes of something as boring as a democratically chosen Water Board. Let alone that they would want to exert influence on policy. Nevertheless, the work of the Water Boards is of vital importance for everyone in the Netherlands. If they were to stop pumping, a large part of the Netherlands would soon be under water again. They have to keep bailing out water every day to keep everyone's feet dry.

The Water Boards are responsible for maintaining the water level, but to achieve this they are dependent on the climate conditions of the moment. The Dike Reeves do not

THE WATER BOARD REPRESENTS A HUGELY UNDERESTIMATED POWER FACTOR

know either what is going to happen in the future. In the last decade, they have certainly been faced with the facts a few times: the polder system has become very vulnerable because of the steadily reducing flexibility in water levels. The West-land, a polder region between The Hague and Rotterdam, had to deal with a large amount of rain in 1996. The water could not be sufficiently drained off. In some of the polders, there was around 30 cm of water. That may not sound like very much, but if your business or house is affected, the damage is enormous.

Farmers are another important party in decisions about spatial structure. They have control of a large part of

A large percentage of the agricultural acreage in the western Netherlands is taken up by greenhouses. This intensive form of agriculture cannot cope with much fluctuation in the water level in the polders.

Nieuwerkerk, the island of Schouwen Duiveland (left). The Flood Disaster took place during the night of 31 January/1 February 1953. Spring tide and a north-westerly storm drove the water of the North Sea to a record height. Large areas in the south-west of the Netherlands were flooded after the dikes collapsed (right). More than 1,800 people and many animals drowned; 100,000 people lost their homes and possessions. There were also floods in England, Belgium and Germany with hundreds of victims. The disaster was the pretext for the Delta Works, which included the closure of several sea arms by means of enormous storm surge barriers and dams.

the Netherlands. A century ago, regular adjustments to the water level for farmers was everyday reality. In the past, the polder worked like a sponge: in the winter a little more water could be absorbed, in the summer a little less. These days, farmers are increasingly reluctant to accept a landscape with constantly fluctuating levels, because that has a negative effect on the rationalized running of their business. A constant water level is important, particularly for the greenhouse farming sector, which has expanded dramatically in the last decades. That is why the choice was made in the 1960s, under pressure from the agricultural sector, to increasingly fix the water levels in the polders. For the Water Boards, all that pumping is no problem at all. They can easily handle a more regular water level. They moved from windmills to electric pumping to increase capacity. This means that they can regulate levels with previously unheard-of precision.

New Land

All the power factors, from the interests of the farmers to the hidden policy of the District Water Boards, have largely led to the disappearance of spatial dynamism in the Netherlands. That wasn't always the case. In 1953, there was a huge flood disaster in the Netherlands. During the night of 31 January/1 February, spring tide and a north-westerly storm drove the water of the North Sea to a record height. Large parts of the provinces of Zeeland, West-Brabant and the Zuid-Holland islands were flooded. More than 1,800 people and a large number of animals drowned. Over 100,000 people lost their homes and possessions. This disaster occasioned

Flood Disaster 1953. Aerial photo of the dike collapse at Den Bommel on the island of Goeree Overflakkee, taken on 1 February 1953.

(Left)
Storm surge barrier in the Eastern Scheldt, which can be closed when floods occur; it keeps land below sea level safe during storms. At the front, the high black solid dike that protects the land against the sea.

(Right)
Maeslant storm barrier in the Nieuwe Waterweg (New Waterway). During threats of flooding from the sea, two gigantic doors close off the Nieuwe Waterweg. In this way, South Holland is protected from critically high tides. This flood barrier is almost as long as the Eiffel Tower in Paris is high, and is even four times as heavy.

the construction of the largest water works ever built in the Netherlands: the Delta Works. By placing massive storm surge barriers between the islands in Zeeland, the coastline of the Netherlands was shortened by 700 km. Showpieces are, even now, the Eastern Scheldt and Maeslandt flood barriers. Even earlier, in 1918, after a flood disaster in 1916, the Dutch Lower House passed the Zuiderzee Act. This provided for the construction of the Afsluitdijk, separating the North Sea from the Zuiderzee and, in so doing, creating the IJsselmeer. The last gap in the more than 30-km-long dike was closed in 1932.

Now that the wild Zuiderzee had been transformed into a peaceful lake, the Dutch authorities decided to build Flevoland and the Noordoostpolder, to provide a solution to the growing need for space. Once the last, most southerly area of Flevoland was drained in 1968, almost 1,500 km² of new land had been extracted from the water. As though it were the most normal thing in the world, the Netherlands had added 5 per cent to its own territory, completely peacefully, by using civil engineering works. The energetic way in which these works were tackled was unprecedented. A few young men, still in their thirties, graduates of the Universities of Technology, sat round the table and worked out how to carry out these unbelievable works. Naturally, they paid good attention to the risks, but if they had been faced with the current requirement to completely preclude every single risk involved in each spatial intervention, the Delta Works and the IJsselmeer would never have been achieved.

The 32-km-long Afsluitdijk closes off the IJsselmeer (the former Zuiderzee) from the Wadden Sea. Construction began in 1927; the final gap was closed in 1932. The inland sea created was suitable for large-scale land reclamation. The result was Flevoland: 1,500 km2 of new land and the youngest province in the Netherlands.

The polder system, with all its dikes, canals and pumping stations, sits in Dutch genes. However, impoldering does have a downside; it has quite a few faults. In relation to what it yields, they are only small imperfections, but still important enough to mention and to see what can be done about them.

Flooding Risk

The most important shortcoming of the polder is the danger of flooding. The risk of flooding is the product of the chance of flooding and the consequences flooding can have, expressed in personal victims and economic damage. The chance of flooding can be determined for the relevant dikes in a particular area by calculating load (water levels and waves) and strength (height and ground construction of the flood barrier). The risk is subsequently calculated, based on the number of inhabitants and the economic production of the area in question. Based on the risk, the safety norms for the area are assessed, and using that as foundation, the required strength of the dikes is determined. The rings of dikes around the islands in Zeeland in the south-west of the Netherlands, for example, are constructed in such a way that catastrophic flooding will take place on average once every 4,000 years. That does not seem very often, but imagine if you have just moved there when the flooding takes place. The highest safety norms can be found in the provinces Noord- and Zuid-Holland, where Amsterdam, Rotterdam and The Hague are situated. In those areas, catastrophic flooding is calculated to take place once every 10,000 years. The lowest safety norms apply to the areas bordering the major rivers; they are allowed to be under water once every 1,250 years. So in the Netherlands, the risk of flooding is the result of conscious economic and political choices. The choices made do not work out equally positively for every inhabitant.

Saline Seepage

Another problem is saline seepage. Saline seepage happens when sea water seeps into the surface water via the subsoil. This is a problem because the salinity of the groundwater interferes with agriculture. Polders make the problem of saline seepage worse. The edge of the above-mentioned Haarlemmermeer Polder, for instance, is less than 10 km from the North Sea. In simple terms: the fresh water pumped out of the polder every day, comes up again on the other side in the form of salty seawater. The sea and the polder work as two communicating vessels. The harder you pump, the faster the saltwater moves into the area. As a result, the ground is salinized and the area becomes increasingly unsuitable for agriculture.

Sinking Land

Besides saline seepage, there is also the problem of sinking land. Draining polders causes the ground to settle. This phenomenon is called shrinkage. It leads to increasing ground subsidence, with the result that the polders are situated lower and lower. The low regions of the Netherlands subside more and more as a consequence. Naturally, that is not convenient: the more the polder sinks, the stronger the surrounding dikes need to be and the worse the saline seepage becomes.

Rotting Peat Landscape

In the Netherlands, the need to reduce CO_2 emissions has filtered through to every layer of society. Insulating houses, limiting the amount of waste and more economical cars should reduce the contribution of the Netherlands to the greenhouse effect. These are all reductions directly related to consumer use. However, the artificial landscape in the Netherlands makes a significant contribution to CO_2 production as well. That happens via evaporation: the oxidation of peat grounds that have been drained and are now dry as a result. When dry peat comes in contact with oxygen, a biological decomposition process occurs, during which large amounts of CO_2 are released. These emissions must be added to the emissions caused by all the pumping stations. The decay of peat alone amounts for approximately 3 per cent of the total annual emissions of CO_2 in the Netherlands. That is equivalent to the annual CO_2 emissions of around three million cars. If no action is taken, emissions are expected to rise to one-and-a-half to two times the current level.

As it turns out, the problem with peat oxidation is not exclusive to the Netherlands: it happens in other parts of the world on an even larger scale. In 2006, research carried out by NGO Wetlands International and Delft Hydraulics

THE MOST IMPORTANT SHORTCOMING OF THE POLDER IS THE DANGER OF FLOODING

demonstrated that the dehydration and destruction of peat grounds in Indonesia had had a 'shocking influence' on the greenhouse effect worldwide. Measurements carried out by Delft Hydraulics showed that Indonesian peat on Sumatra and Kalimantan is responsible for the emission of 2,000 million tons (2 billion kg) of CO_2. That means that 'greenhouse' gas emissions by Indonesia are three times the amount produced by the whole of Germany. The figure is also higher than countries such as India and Russia. These figures put Indonesia in third place on the list of 'most-greenhouse-gas-producing' countries, immediately behind the USA and China. Before these calculations came to light, Indonesia was in 21st place on this list.[20]

NEW WATER MOVEMENT

So the polder system is far from perfect. The disadvantages are hardly insignificant: land settles, the ground becomes more salty and it takes a lot of effort to keep it dry. Furthermore, the safety of people living in polders is reducing due to the rising level of the sea. In spite of this, not much action is being taken. The urgency and optimism that surrounded the construction of the Delta Works and the Afsluitdijk and the reclamation of Flevoland have disappeared like snow in summer. It has run out of steam. Everyone is concerned about future climate change but is behaving like a frightened rabbit caught in the headlights of an approaching car, instead of taking control and anticipating what is going to happen.

There is an alternative and that is looking at ways of dealing with water innovatively. The first initiative is this direction is the New Water Movement. The basic principle behind this movement is the transformation from static to dynamic polders. In fact, fluctuating water levels provide an answer to the current problems with the polders, climate change and the pressure exerted by urbanization on the polder landscape. For instance, ground water expert Gualbert Oude Essink of research institute Deltares has a clear solution for the problem of saline seepage in the Haarlemmermeer. He says, let the Haarlemmermeer fill up with fresh water. Not immediately, of course. No, think about it now and allow people to get used to the idea. Then you can open the sluice gates 70 years from now. The benefits outweigh the disadvantages. In March 2005 in the Dutch newspaper *Trouw*, he said: 'As a groundwater expert I look at the fresh water that could be stored in the middle of the Randstad. It would be a buffer against advancing salt water. In this way, you could make large parts of the groundwater in the surrounding land useable. Now it is brackish, it threatens fresh water facilities and disrupts agriculture.'

In the long run, most farmers will have to leave the Haarlemmermeer, either because of salinization or because the Haarlemmermeer sinks under water. Naturally, inundating the polder has far-reaching consequences: 140,000 people live in the area and four motorways pass through it. Schiphol would also have to relocate: 'To an island off the coast in the North Sea. Everything would need to be well-prepared to ensure, for example, that no undesirable changes in sea currents are caused. But an airport in the sea could contribute to the defence of the coast. Higher sea levels lead to higher waves and they can be broken by an island off the coast. If parts of the airport are constructed under sea level, that can attract brackish or saline groundwater that would otherwise stream inland.' It is a question of thinking outside the box: 'If we restrict ourselves to more of what we do already, in a few decades we could be too late for considered preparations. That is why we need to start now.'[21]

The New Water Movement not only provides a solution to the problems mentioned above, at the same time it is a new foundation for urban functions. A flexible water level in the polders, also known as 'depolderization', is the only correct next step for water management in the Netherlands. There is a lot of resistance to depolderization, particularly among farmers. The situation is illustrated by the endless arguments about depolderizing the Hertogin Hedwige Polder in Zeeland, a decision taken by the Dutch parliament in 2009. Opponents consider it against the nature of the Dutch people to 'give land back to the sea'. But the New Water Movement has nothing to do with giving the Netherlands back to the sea. It is about the eminently sensible choice to make the polder system more flexible by draining less. In this way, the Netherlands would become less artificial and the spatial structure would do more justice to the subsoil.

Depolderization is a broad concept with many faces. The wet polder, the filled polder and the polder as water column, for instance.

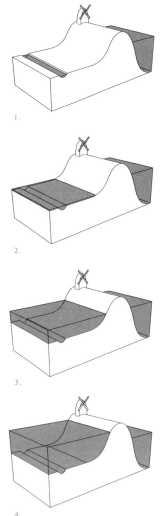

The drained polder (1) and three possible forms of depolderization: the wet polder (2), the filled polder (3) and the polder as water column (4).

Wet Polder

In a wet polder, the water level is only raised slightly, so that the land is only just under water. The water level in a standard polder is often only 20 to 30 cm below dry ground. The step to a wet polder can therefore be achieved with a change in water level of just 50 cm. This brings the settling and decomposition of the peat landscape to a halt.

Filled Polder

A little more drastic than a wet polder is to bring the water level in a polder to boezem level. The *boezem* is the higher-lying canal round the polder. This *boezem* is intended to periodically collect polder water and drain it away to open water. The polder dike remains intact in this variant. There is no longer a difference in water level between the polder and the surrounding boezem, that is all. That makes it a filled polder.

Polder as Water Column

At the other end of the spectrum, there is also the possibility to raise the polder dike on the inside by metres, to make the polder level higher than the *boezem* level. This would provide opportunities for concentrated water storage in polder cells. It would raise the pressure on the salt water and drive back saline seepage.

New Water in Westland, the Netherlands

One example of a sustainable and innovative way of dealing with the polders is 'The New Water' in the Poel Polder in the municipality of Westland, which is being transformed for this purpose into a filled polder. The project, designed by Waterstudio, is advanced in the areas of ecology, urban design and architecture, with various water-bound or water-related types of housing. The ambition is to create a high-quality residential building location that gives an idea of living in future depolderized landscapes in the Netherlands.

The New Water offers an alternative view of the traditional polder system: instead of continual drainage, it allows water space in certain places. For the client, development company Het Nieuwe Westland (ONW), the starting point was permanent depolderization, instead of occasionally inundating the polder, as happens now in water storage areas. The idea is a permanently higher water level, with the possibility of adding even more water in situations where extra collection capacity is required. Waterstudio was approached for the project because of their years of expertise with economically viable plans for floating houses. The concepts for buoyant houses developed in previous years were ready to be used in an integrated vision for the area.

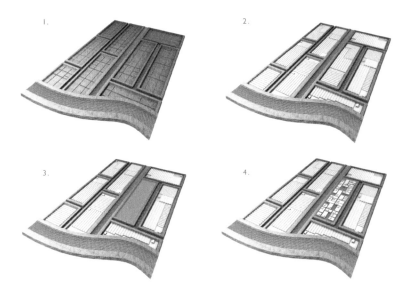

The principle of
depolderization.

1. The polders before the
arrival of the greenhous-
es, when small fluctua-
tions in water levels were
still possible.
2. The polders after the arrival of the greenhouses,
with the consequence
that fluctuations in water
levels were hardly pos-
sible at all.
3. A single polder has been
depolderized and acts
as water collection, to
absorb temporary peaks
in the water load (for
instance due to heavy
rainfall or a high water
level in the rivers).
4. After the housing is complete, the polder will be
flooded again, so that the
platform can float.

What makes this project special, apart from its appearance, is the collaboration in a public-private partnership of a
number of parties who would previously have had conflicting
interests: the Water Control Board is responsible for keeping
the area dry by supplying water storage, the province of
South Holland is responsible for maintaining and developing
the infrastructure and ecological structures, the municipality
of Westland would like extra new-build while the Dutch
Municipalities Bank (BNG) wants to develop the region.
Although there are some conflicts of interest in the limited
space of the traditional polder system, the water here creates
a collective interest. Depolderization means that all the wishes
can be united in a single area, but apart from that, all the
parties together are necessary. The space needed by the
Water Control Board for water collection would hardly be
realizable if it could not also be used for building houses;
similarly, the ecological structure could not be continued
in an area dominated mainly by greenhouse farming.

As a result, The New Water is an experimental field
for durable solutions, not just in terms of spatial design but
also in the collaboration of all the parties involved. In the
coming years, the plan will form the blueprint for water
collection areas where housing development, ecology and
water management are integrated – the polder 2.0.

By depolderization and making use of floating functions, double use is made of the land. In a region where intensive greenhouse farming is the economic motor, while housing

The New Water Project, designed by Waterstudio, is a largely floating new-build residential development in the Westland region of South Holland. The former polder will be set under water and provides room for water collection, green spaces and housing. The plan provides for different 'rooms', each with their own distinctive identity. One conspicuous component of the plan is the floating apartment complex, The Citadel. The starting point for the design was a mass of rocks where water has carved out channels. The façades will be clad with aluminium shingles, which are sustainable due to their long lifespan and recyclability. The apartments will be 4 m high, including the construction. Parking space is situated in the basement. The foundations consist of a buoyant concrete trough; the underside of the basement floor is 3 m under water level. The structure will be made of steel with wooden floors.

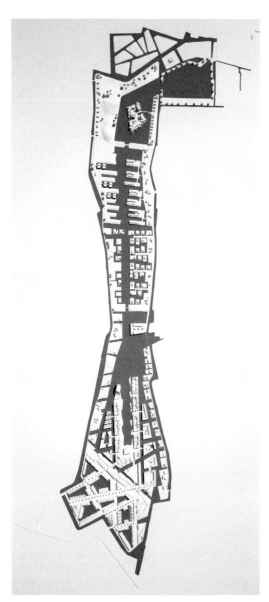

Model of The New
Water Project.

development, ecology and water also require space, sacrificing a small piece of greenhouse area will generate the security that the whole region will be kept dry.

The New Water project demonstrates what is possible when the rigid line of reasoning about polders is abandoned. The spatial structure of the Netherlands is not a static fact. In the same way that innovation, creativity and determination led to impressive civil engineering works in the past, these characteristics and the latest insights into water can now lead to depolderization. Depolderization is not giving up a cherished identity, but instead the logical next step in the dynamic process of dealing with water. While the Dutch authorities are still in a clinch with farmers about the depolderization of a small piece of extensively used agricultural ground, the country will need to be depolderized on a large scale in the coming years if it wants to keep its feet dry. In rural regions, the polder as a drained bathtub is coming to the end of its time.

Anyone visiting the Netherlands in 50 years time may see a much wetter country. The polder 2.0 is entering a thriving time: lower drainage costs, increased safety and a more visible and understandable system for the inhabitants. Polders filled with water, where urban design, agricultural activities, infrastructure and ecology are integrated into water storage areas, will provide architects and urban designers with a challenge to come up with new concepts that do justice to the artificial experiment known as the Netherlands.

IMAGIN

ING FLC

ATING

GREENE

RY

Island of Manhattan, NYC
skyscrapers receding from
view above the wake of a
ferry

Chapter 6

FLOATING LANDSCAPES

Imagine for a moment: you have lived in New York for years. Now and again you take the ferry to Staten Island, to visit the Maritime Museum in the lovely buildings in Snug Harbor, for example. On the way there, you always pass three islands: Liberty Island, with its famous Statue, Governors Island and Ellis Island, where immigrants first set foot on American soil from 1892 onwards. But now, right in front of the ship's bows, you see a fourth island with grassy hills, trees and even a beach. Is it a fata morgana? Could be, if you haven't eaten enough for days. But it could also be a floating island, towed there within the last 24 hours. To create space for a golf course near the city centre. Or perhaps a beach or a public park.

Rigidity

Floating landscapes are flexible buoyant constructions, that move with the rhythm of the waves in the water and that are planted with vegetation and trees. These types of construction offer a whole range of possibilities that go beyond the floating concrete platforms that have been covered up to now. After all, completely rigid platforms are not necessary for floating islands if they do not have to support heavy buildings. There is a linear relationship between rigidity and building costs: the more rigid the platform, the more expensive it is. Buildings are worth money and, as a result, rigid foundations soon become cost-effective, but for functions that cost more than they bring in, flexible floating foundations are a good option. For instance, functions consisting of only a few buildings or none at all, such as floating nature, recreation areas, agriculture and drinking water storage.

A schematic sketch by Watersturio for the flexible connection of various platforms for a floating city district. Instead of making large platforms that are completely stable in their own right, the whole construction can also be made stable by coupling smaller elements. The bridges function in this situation as hinges and absorb vertical thrust. In this way, the platforms form links that act as counterweights to cushion each other's movements.

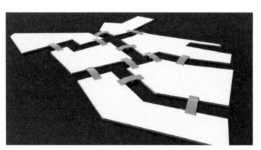

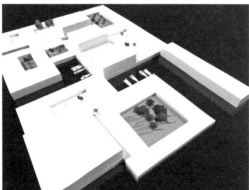

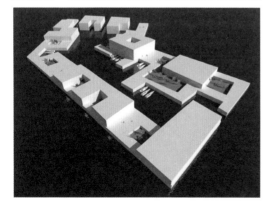

Flexible floating foundations are called non-rigids. They are islands that move with the water on which they float, due to the characteristics of the material used to construct them. That can be either natural or synthetic materials. Floating mattresses of synthetic material could be fabricated from recycled plastic, for example, originating from old sports shoes and mattresses that have been pulverized and melted together. Such bases are already widely used in geotechnological applications and as drainage mats underneath waste processing installations. They are buoyant, robust and sustainable.

An intermediate form between rigid foundations and non-rigids are the semi-rigids. Including flexible hinges between rigid platforms makes them stiffer than non-rigids but not as stiff as rigids. The degree of rigidity depends on the function you have in mind. If someone walks over a floating mattress, the load is negligible, so a non-rigid will not

Spiral Island 2 boasts a wishing well, hammock, beaches, dwelling and rooftop balcony.

move either in this situation. If an enormous storm blows up and the island begins to bob a little, that is not a problem in many cases. So it is not necessary to spend a disproportionate amount of money to make the foundations completely rigid.

A fantastic example of a non-rigid made from recycled plastic is eco-pioneer Richart ('Rishi') Sowa's Spiral Island; it floats on thousands of empty plastic bottles. His desire for a simpler existence led Sowa, a carpenter in daily life, to give up his job, family and possessions in Great Britain and

Spiral Island off the coast.

move to South America. His dream was to live on an uninhabited island. Because there was a shortage of unin-habited islands, in the end he decided to make one himself. He began building the first version in 1998 near Puerto Aventuras, off the coast of Mexico to the south of Cancún. He used floating nets filled with empty plastic bottles as the foundation for a construction of plywood and bamboo, upon which he

Rishi Sowa in front of his Spiral Island 2, the new and as yet modest version of Spiral Island 1. He built the new island in 2007 and 2008 close to Isla Mujeres, near Cancún, after the previous larger island was destroyed by hurricane Emily in 2005.

dumped sand. His Spiral Island, approximately 20 m in diameter, provided space for a two-storey house, a self-composting toilet and several beaches. He was virtually completely self-sufficient; banana, coconut and almond trees and tomato plants provided his daily food.

Sowa's ambition was to let his island continue to grow and ultimately, once it was large enough, to head out onto the deep blue sea and sail the world on his private little paradise. The island managed to survive two hurricanes and several tropical storms, but was destroyed in 2005 by hurricane Emily. However, Sowa did not abandon his dream and he built a new Spiral Island in 2007 and 2008 in the waters of Isla Mujeres, also nearby Cancún. The new Spiral Island has a diameter of roughly 20 m as well and is covered with plants and mangroves, just like the previous version. Approximately 100,000 plastic bottles provide sufficient buoyancy. As a result, the island can support a house, two pools, a solar-powered waterfall and a large number of solar panels. 'One day, we will sail out onto the ocean and become a small floating country,' says Sowa in a video on his own website. [22]

Natural Floating Landscapes

Floating landscapes are not new. In fact, they are a regular feature in nature. In the form of floating peat islands, for instance. Peat landscapes cover a large part of the Netherlands. This type of artificially formed landscape is found nowhere else on earth, unless it has been installed by Dutch people as an export product, in the English Fens and Somerset Levels, for example. Cornelius Wasterdyk Vermuyden (1595-1677) introduced Dutch inpoldering methods there, complete with polder locks, ring canals, windmills, sluices and pumping stations. The Dutch were involved right from the start of peat reclamation development in Germany, Denmark, France, Italy and Poland.

Floating peat islands are created when a peat layer is submerged and subsequently comes loose from the bottom. That can happen either spontaneously or by human intervention. The latter is what happened in the Dutch region of Goudbergven, for example. The Goudberg region is part of the Strijbeekse Heide nature reserve. In the middle is the Patersmoer, a peat marsh enclosed by a dune. To reclaim the peatlands, a drainage ditch was dug and dammed up in 1959. The water level then rose by a metre, which resulted in a floating *drijftil* – cluster of peat – breaking free from its surroundings. Since then, there is a floating peat island with a surface area of around 1.5 hectares in a so-called 'ring fen'.

In the Netherlands there are only a few fens with a floating peat island like this, but they do exist elsewhere in Europe. In the Russian Rybinsk reservoir, for instance. This artificial lake is a large water reservoir on the Volga. The shores of the lake are low-lying and there are pastures, woods and marshes in various places. On the north-western shore there are large amounts of overgrown peat, which regularly break free from the shore to create floating peat islands. These islands float over the whole reservoir now and represent valuable mini-biosystems.

Then there are the floating peat islands in Montenegro, in the Skadar lake, near the border with Albania. This lake, which is on Unesco's Ramsar List of Wetlands, is one of the largest bird reserves in Europe and contains an enormous biodiversity. It is surrounded by marshlands and floating peat islands, particularly in the north-western corner.

Floating ecology is also important for urban landscapes. In the Netherlands, the placing and maintaining of ecological structures makes up a significant part of spatial planning. In a country where water takes up a large part of the surface area and urbanization with its corresponding asphalt exerts significant pressure on the use of space, floating greenery on water can make an important contribution to the quality of life, for people as well as animals.

Building on Floating Landscapes

Some cultures have been building on floating islands made of natural materials for centuries. The Uros Indians in Peru and Bolivia, for instance. They live on floating reed islands on Lake Titicaca. The basis of the islands is formed by blocks of compact reed roots, taken from the lake. These blocks are connected and anchored to the bottom with ropes and poles. Woven reed mats, knotted together in large numbers, are laid on top. If the number of families on an island gets too large, the inhabitants simply saw the island in half and let the sawn-off half drift a little further away. The islands are not rigid; if you walk over them you sink a little into the soft reed, and when there are waves, they bob noticeably. Nonetheless, the islands are sufficiently buoyant to be built on; not just with houses but also with an occasional watchtower.

Because the islands rot away on the underside from lying in water, the Indians fill the floating mats from the top at regular intervals. This method of working does give rise to a few problems. The quality of the water near the islands deteriorates rapidly due to the continuous process of rotting, and climate change has meant that there is insufficient growth of new reed. The floating communities will probably disappear in time as a result. But this sort of vernacular can inspire new developments in the West. If these people, with their limited resources, can build a floating island with very light materials on top, then others must also be capable of achieving that with their technological know-how.

It is possible to build floating peat islands with light-weight constructions. The Dutch knew that as long ago as the seventeenth century. When Maria de Medici, the mother of the French King Louis XIII visited Amsterdam on Tuesday 31 August 1638, the city was in a state of commotion. So many cannon salutes were fired that there were thick smoke clouds hanging over the city. Four thousand soldiers lined the route taken by the royal carriage. The 63 year-old French queen mother was treated to three days of festivities. Friday was the highlight of her visit. In a single night, a triumphal arch was built on a floating peat island in the Rokin, 'as large as an entire house', according to accounts of the event.[23]

The floating islands on Lake Titicaca are home to the Uros Indians.

Floating Green

Many metropolises have a shortage of parks and public space. Parks are important, because they absorb water and give it back to the air slowly through evaporation. Cities that only have asphalt and brick, and where excess water is drained off via the sewage system, have an unhealthy living climate; the air is dry there. As a result, there are a lot of fine particles in the atmosphere. The consequence is that many city dwellers have breathing difficulties. In addition, the sewage system alone often cannot handle heavy rainfall; as a result, dry cities are paradoxically often plagued with flooding during a rainy period. Parks, green roofs and other green spaces provide an even moisture balance. Furthermore, parks improve the quality of living and this has a positive effect on the value of the surrounding properties. It is no coincidence that the most expensive houses in cities are often on the edges of parks, for instance Upper Eastside near Central Park in New York, Oud-Zuid near the Vondel Park in Amsterdam, and Knightsbridge and Belgravia near Hyde Park in London.

Arie Voorburg, senior advisor in urban development at engineering firm Arcadis, has carried out extensive research into the role of green spaces in large cities. His conclusions

When Maria de Medici visited Amsterdam in 1638, a triumphal arch was constructed on a floating peat island on Rokin, 'as large as an entire house'. Print made by S. Savrij (etcher), Simon de Vlieger (artist) and Salomon Savery (etcher), 1638, Amsterdam City Archive, Atlas Dreesmann Collection.

An example of the 'trading places' strategy – the design for a floating city boulevard in Miami. As the price of land rises in the centre, public space often comes under pressure from economic development. By relocating this type of function to the waterline, space frees up in the centre for economically cost-effective developments and the waterside is given a positive impulse at the same time. Furthermore, functions such as sports fields, boulevards and parks can be realized simply and cheaply as floating elements, due to the low mechanical load and large surface area.

about the negative influence of too few parks on the climate of the city go one step further. To clarify his point, he uses the concept of heat stress: the phenomenon that many cities are literally overheated. In his opinion, many metropolitan districts and streets are not equipped for a changing climate. The rise in temperature has direct consequences for the liveability of these cities. The warmth radiated by buildings and asphalt is an oppressive and even dangerous heat. By an average rise in temperature of three degrees in 2050, it could easily be 10 to 20 degrees warmer in the city, according to Voorburg. Further densification of existing building stock in inner cities is therefore not a good option, as far as he is concerned. Work productivity drops, the number of people with chronic illnesses increases as well as aggression, criminality and mortality rates: all characteristics of badly designed and built metropolises. Voorburg is convinced that cities have to be able to 'air'. Trees, roof gardens and façades with growing plants retain water and provide shade and liveability. Floating parks supply room for all the green facilities required to keep metropolises healthy.[24]

Design by Unit1 for a floating hydroponic pavilion in Turku, Finland. Hydroponics is a method of growing plants without soil, using mineral nutrient solutions in water. The pavilion functions as an experimental water reactor, in which water from the River Aura is extracted and isolated in a closed basin where algae cultures act as cleaning agents.

Floating green landscapes represent a huge potential for improving a city's visual image. Floating boulevards, parks and beaches restore the relationship between water and city in places where that contact has disappeared, due to the construction of roads or railway lines, for instance. But also in ecological terms, floating landscapes make an important contribution to the existing city. They can replace facilities such as public green spaces and sports fields situated on expensive inner-city ground, thereby freeing up those locations for building works. In this way, floating parks can be made cost-effective. Furthermore, floating green landscapes can be interchanged depending on the season, just like a vase of flowers. The same has been happening since time immemorial with the terrace boats in the canals of Amsterdam; they are removed in the winter.

Floating gardens in an urban setting are nothing new. The Dutch company Nautilus makes floating green quaysides, called Aqua-Flora Floats, which can be found in various places on the Amsterdam canals. The company is currently building a 4-km^2 floating nursery for an eco-city in China, which should not only make a visual contribution to the city but also serve as a water purification facility. The nursery will contain 20 different sorts of plants suitable for fresh water (up to 800 mg

New Amsterdam Park is a design for a public domain on the waters of the IJ River. A fleet of large re-used barges can now be found where huge sea vessels once lay at anchor. The design by Rietveld Landscape and Atelier de Lyon is inspired by both the problem of flood tides and the protracted debate about the construction of a permanent park island near KNSM Island. The temporary floating park makes use of the space that will be available for the next decade until the permanent park island is constructed. After that, it can be moored somewhere else along the banks of the IJ.

of salt per litre of water), brackish water (800-2000 mg per litre) and salt water (anything above 2000 mg per litre). Since 2000 there has been a 10 x 20-m floating garden in the Entrepôt Harbour in Amsterdam, designed by the artist Robert Jasper Grootveld. The garden is not open to the public, so nature has been given free rein for the last decade, and that has resulted in a piece of wilderness in the middle of the strictly planned buildings in the Eastern Harbour area. Many houseboats in the city are also equipped with floating gardens, which are usually quite small, however, due to the restrictions stipulated in the land use plan.

The exhibition 'Architecture of Consequence', which could be seen from February to May 2010 in the Netherlands Architecture Institute, demonstrated that floating landscapes on a larger scale in Amsterdam are being investigated as a serious alternative to green facilities on land. The Amsterdam Waterexpo foundation commissioned Rietveld Landscape and Atelier de Lyon to design a temporary floating park on the River IJ. The pretexts for the design are the requirement for a jetty for inland shipping, the sailing event Sail 2010 and the

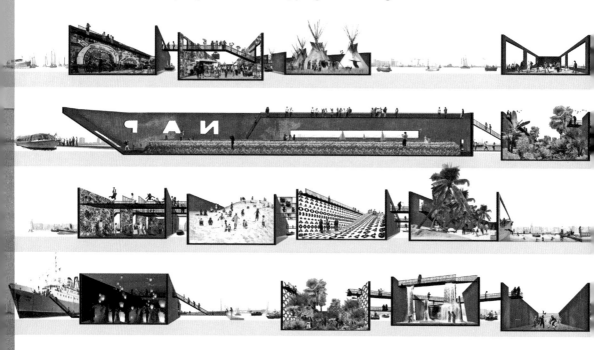

issue of the construction of a permanent park island on the same spot; this issue has been dragging on for years.

Instead of a static park island, Rietveld Landscape and Atelier de Lyon have suggested constructing a flexible version that moves with the rhythm of the water. New Amsterdam Park (NAP) would give the inhabitants of the city the opportunity to experience the rough beauty of the harbour and provide the city with an exciting new public domain. A grid consisting of roughly 30 tug-pushed lighters (90 x 11.4 x 5.5 m apiece) provides shelter for a hidden water world on the IJ. There is always contact with the vastness of the IJ and the Dutch cloudscapes because many park elements, such as grassy

Floating Gardens is a design for a Spa and Wellness Centre in the Amsterdam district of IJburg. The plan makes use of botanist Patrick Blanc's Living Walls, constructed from the composite GreenRexwall that Blanc developed in collaboration with German builder Aquahouse. The hydroponic composite, which consists mainly of re-used polystyrene, is strong enough to function as brick, has a high insulation value and is very buoyant.

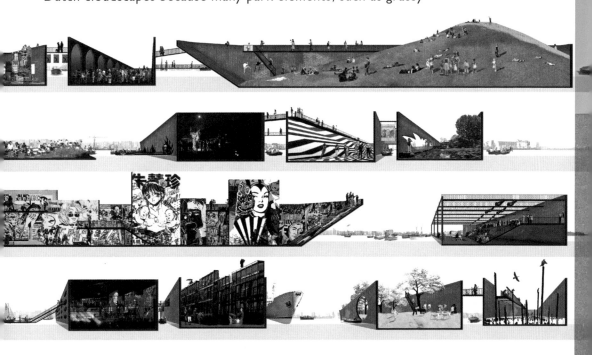

hills, protrude above the barges. The floating lighters generate flexibility to allow shrinkage or expansion. NAP can be reached by public transport over water or with your own boat.

The other design seen at the exhibition was created by the architects Anne Holtrop and Roderick van der Weijden, and the developers Studio Noach and botanist Patrick Leblanc, and is for a floating spa garden in IJburg, a new neighbourhood on artificially filled-in islands on the IJ. The floating building, which accommodates baths, saunas and several terraces, is covered with plants from Patrick Blanc's Living Walls. This system uses recycled polystyrene instead of soil. Water with sufficient minerals and nutrients, daylight and carbon dioxide are enough to get the process of photosynthesis going. The fresh water from the IJ acts as a heat exchanger. It also serves as a source of warmth and cooling and is 70 per cent more energy-saving than conventional energy facilities as a result.

It is not just the existing city that has much to gain by the introduction of more green spaces; the current genera-tion of water houses can benefit from floating greenery. Many water neighbourhoods are bare affairs, jetty landscapes with floating houses without any atmosphere. Floating gardens can be entirely prefabricated, by allowing them to grow at another location and sailing them in when the neighbourhood is com-pleted. That would give water neighbourhoods an immediately mature appearance.

Floating Golf Course

On a larger scale altogether, and closer to realization, is the floating golf course designed by Waterstudio and Dutch Docklands for the Maldives, where the highest point is only 2 m above sea level. In March 2010, the island nation signed a deal with Dutch Docklands International to develop building the world's first permanent floating golf course, together with a convention centre and residential rooms, on a platform in the Indian Ocean.

The project could act as a pioneer for floating villages and towns, Mahmood Razee, the Minister for Civil Aviation, Communication and Privatization, told *The Times*. 'If it is suc-cessful, we will try to work with them to see if they could develop housing facilities as well... We need this because of climate change and because island erosion has caused a shortage of land.'

President Mohammed Nasheed of the Maldives has made his country the poster child for the risks of rising sea levels due to climate change, *The Times* article continues. He said he will make it the first carbon neutral country by 2020 and may create a sovereign wealth fund to buy land in case the Maldives becomes uninhabitable. In October 2009, the Cabinet staged a meeting – complete with desks – in scuba gear on the seabed to highlight the dangers of global warming.

Yet the threat of flooding is an everyday reality for Maldivians as well as the stuff of publicity stunts; the capital, Malé, is protected by a 30-million-dollar sea wall and many islands are experiencing severe beach erosion. After the 2004 tsunami, which killed more than 100 people in the Maldives, the coral base of one island was destroyed, forcing its community to relocate. Of the 90,000 km^2 the country covers, the vast majority is water.

If the golf course is realized, the Maldives Government hopes that it will attract more business tourists in the short term, to add to the hundreds of thousands of visitors who flock there each year. It will be permanently anchored in Malé atoll, the central group of coral islands, and will be designed to have minimal environmental impact. According to a statement from the Maldivian President's office: 'Procedures developed by the company for floating developments reduce the impact on underwater life, and minimise the changes to coastal morphology.'

Impression of a floating golf course by Waterstudio and Dutch Docklands for the Maldives. The island has an organic form; luxury holiday homes with their own private beach are located in the bays. A golf course has a relatively small load, spread over a large surface area, so it is ideal to implement this function as a semi-rigid construction. In addition, the island is not completely rigid but works like a large flexible mattress that absorbs the pressure from the waves.

The atoll already has one artificial island reclaimed from the sea, Hulhumalé, which spans 188 hectares and was completed in 2004. It was built to reduce pressure on Malé Island, which accommodates 100,000 people on a single square mile.[25]

Floating Food

Floating landscapes can also provide a solution to current problems outside the city, in the form of floating agriculture, for example, or even floating salt farming. The floating greenhouses in the Dutch town of Naaldwijk, completed on 7 September 2005 by construction company Dura Vermeer, were mentioned briefly in chapter 2. Floating greenhouses make it possible to combine intensive greenhouse farming and water collection. There is certainly a requirement for this sort of clustering, because space in the Netherlands is limited while the demand for living, working and leisure activities is rising. In the coming years, many tens of thousands of hectares will be organized for water collection, at the expense of the available ground space. By giving each of these water collection areas an extra function, it would be easier to create room for water.

Agriculture, however, together with its corresponding requirement for water facilities, has a much greater problem to deal with: the growing world population and generally increasing farming productivity have a serious effect on fresh water reserves, which eventually become salty due to evaporation and rainfall. The more water evaporates from farming areas, the more saline agricultural land becomes; after all, the salt present in the ground does not evaporate along with the water. The process by which salty agricultural land develops is irreversible in dry areas, and therefore in developing countries in particular. There are millions of hectares of white-dusted agricultural land that yield little or nothing any more. Brackish land can be found mainly in North Africa, the Middle East, the Indus Valley, Central China and in Uzbekistan and Kazakhstan. Worldwide it concerns 90 million hectares and that area is rising annually with 2 to 4 million hectares.

(Left)
The Greenstar, a design by Watertudio and Dutch Docklands for a floating hotel. The plan consists of five 'arms' with beaches in between. The entire construction is composed of terraces with growing plants, set increasingly further back moving upwards, so it looks like a natural green island that fits into the surroundings. Height differences create a roof landscape that provides space for golf courses, walking routes, swimming pools, restaurants and bars.

(Right)
Between two arms of the Greenstar is a closed channel leading to the inner harbour. Visitors sail under the terraces with growing plants through an almost natural-looking lagoon where small boats can moor and where the entrance to the hotel is located. On the outside, people can walk around the island over paths and beaches.

Due to the increasing scarcity of fresh water and the silting-up of the ground, opportunities for saline agriculture are dawning. Not just in the tropics, but also in more temperate climates. Saline seepage is a growing problem in agricultural areas there, because the sea water level is rising and salt water is gradually being absorbed into farming land in the coastal regions as a result.

So there is more than enough reason for extensive research into saline agriculture. This research is taking place at the moment all over the world. Pioneers in this field are NASA scientists Robert Hendricks (Glenn Research Center, Cleveland, Ohio) and Dennis Bushnell (Langley Research Center, Hampton, Virginia). Many crops can live on salt water: marsh samphire and sea lavender are the best-known examples. Biologists call these crops halophytes. Asparagus and fennel can have a certain amount of natural resistance to salt. Grain crops such as spelt and emmer wheat can tolerate salt, as well as barley and beetroot, especially species for animal feed such as mangelwurzel. The salt tolerance of the related sugar beet could be driven up further by plant breeding. A large number of other crops could also be made suitable for saline agriculture by modification.

Saline agriculture can take place in coastal areas, marshes, inland lakes and desert regions with subterranean brackish aquifers. But the most obvious place is directly at sea. The oceans represent

Large parts of the world have become unusable for agriculture due to salinization.

enormous reservoirs of nutrients that are suitable for floating saline agriculture. Research into saline agriculture is new and very much in development. Floating farming with salt water plants is the agriculture of the future.

Floating Fresh Water

Floating water is less strange than it might appear at first. The phenomenon occurs regularly in nature in the form of icebergs: floating masses of frozen fresh water, originating from a glacier or an ice cap. In the pole circles, there are a great many glaciers that reach as far as the sea. When a glacier sinks into the sea, large fragments break off which subsequently drift away. These icebergs are transported by the sea current to warmer regions and can travel a distance of more than 1,000 km before they have completely melted. In the last few years, studies have been carried out in the UAE into the possibilities of towing icebergs to the Middle East and tapping the melting water to use as a drinking water facility. But with a little imagination, you could do much more with it. In 2009, the German designers Sven and Frank Sauer came up with the plan for a floating ice hotel off the coast of Dubai, called Blue Crystal. 'It shows the bright variety of water and its beauty,' according to the designers.[26]

Design by Waterstudio for a floating crystal hotel near Tromsø. Tromsø is one of the most northerly cities in Norway.

CHAPTER 6 | FLOATING LANDSCAPES

The year before, Waterstudio designed a floating crystal hotel for developer Dutch Docklands. The glass construction, which was intended to be located in the fjords near Tromsø in Norway, was shaped like a snowflake. The rooms were to have a spectacular glass roof, so that the northern lights could be admired from bed.

An iceberg continues to drift because the density of ice is 10 per cent less than that of water (roughly 920 kg/m³ for ice compared to circa 1,025 kg/m³ for water). Ice floes can function exceptionally well as transportable fresh water supplies because they can be moved over large distances without melting. One of the largest known ice floes in the world was the B-15, which broke free from the Ross Ice Shelf in Antarctica in March 2000. With a surface area of 11,000 km², it was

ICEBERGS ARE FLOATING MASSES OF FROZEN FRESH WATER

larger than the island of Jamaica. In 2005, the ice floe collided with the Drygalski Ice Tongue, causing a large piece to break off. The ice floe continued to crumble further in the course of time. In November 2006, remnants of B-15 were found near the city of Timaru in New Zealand. In 2010, ten years after the floe broke free, several fragments had still not completely melted.

Floating ice floes are a danger to shipping, because the smaller chunks are invisible to radar. Ice floes can sometimes be a danger to coastal areas as well. In March 2010, the Russian Army used 15 Sukhoi fighter jets and various Mi-8 attack helicopters to bomb the ice floes in the Siberian rivers

Every summer, the banks
of the Seine River are
transformed into the Paris
Plages, complete with
sand, palm trees, parasols
and showers.

Design for a floating beach.
Waterstudio and Dutch
Docklands developed the
principle to be used in the
bay in Dubai. It consists of a
floating beach and a buoyant
breakwater connected to
each other by a mat that
limits sand loss from the
beach. In combination with
floating houses, the beaches
were to form the words of
an Arabian poem.

Ob, Yenisey, Lena and Amur, to prevent the floating ice from blocking the rivers and causing flooding. According to the Ministry of Civil Defence, in this way almost 3,000 settlements and two million people were preserved from floods.[27]

The problem of dwindling fresh water supplies worldwide is not restricted to agriculture, it can also be felt in another area: drinking water facilities. Supplies of fresh water are being further exhausted worldwide, partly because of melting ice: a consequence of global warming. Approximately 1 per cent of all the water on earth is fresh water and another 1 per cent is brackish. The rest is sea water. Humans are now using around half the total fresh water supplies on earth, and good fresh water is becoming increasingly scarce and expensive.

Floating fresh water supplies are one solution. That need not be solely in the form of floating ice. Salt water is heavier than fresh water, which is why you weigh relatively less in salt water than in fresh. Anyone who has ever floated in the Dead Sea between Israel and Jordan has experienced that firsthand. A logical consequence is that a bag filled with fresh water will continue to float at sea without any extra buoyancy. Fresh water, perhaps won from salt water by means of desalination, can therefore be stored and moved in floating units.

Floating Beaches

Beaches are popular places; water is a good way to cool off on warm days. In large metropolises, where the heat in the summer can be even more suffocating than elsewhere, cooling down on hot days is especially welcome. Natural beaches that directly border the centre of a large city are however, rare. The inhabitants of Sydney, Cape Town, Barcelona and Rio de Janeiro are blessed with Bondi Beach, Clifton, Barceloneta and Copacabana, but most city dwellers are not so well catered for.

If you do not have a beach, it is also possible to create one. Parisians have had their Paris Plages since 2002. Every summer, the city council turns a few locations along the Seine into sandy beaches, complete with golden sand, palm trees, hammocks and showers. People were sceptical at first, but now it is an annually recurring spectacular transformation from paving to sand. Paris Plages have also included a floating swimming pool in the Seine the last few years. The concept is copied these days in a large number of other cities, such as Berlin and Rotterdam. Its success reflects the desire of many city dwellers for a public space on the water.

In Dubai, the desire for a beach has also been a huge stimulus for land reclamation. In the space of ten years, the waterfront has grown from roughly 50 km to 1,500 km. Most of this space is beach. However, hardly any of this 1,500 km is freely accessible. A paltry 1 per cent is open to the public; the rest are private beaches.

These beaches are artificial, filled in by large dredging companies using very sharp sand, in an attempt to obtain the most solid possible result. The rounder the grain of sand, the greater the amount of erosion. The disadvantage of filling in a site is the definite and irreversible destruction of the sea bed. Where sand has been positioned, there is no longer any water.

The beaches are not maintenance-free. Depending on the currents and the heaviness of the seas, the beaches have to be reworked every year. That sounds like a lot of effort, but the same is true of many a European beach. The coast of the Netherlands is also subject to erosion; every year, whole chunks of beach have to be filled in.

The floating beaches designed by Dutch Docklands provide solutions to both the ecological destruction of the sea bed and the constant crumbling away of beaches. The patent consists of floating sandboxes with vegetation. There is a buoyant breakwater positioned several dozen metres in front of the floating boxes. In between, a mat is suspended where sand is poured. The sand goes right through the water line, creating a beach. The finest white sand is used.

The white sand used often has a somewhat round grain. But a solid sand covering can still be achieved by means of a hardening process during which bacteria are washed through the sand. This process is called Biogrout and is a method employed by research institute Deltares. The floating beach's profile is the same as that of a normal beach, up to the first sand bank just off the coast. The floating tube marking the end of the beach is both a float and a breakwater. The tube can be adjusted in height by filling it partly with water and partly with air. In this way, the beach can be protected to a greater or lesser degree from overly heavy seas. Dutch Docklands expects to be able to supply a few per cent of the 1,500 km of beach in Dubai with floating beaches.

Floating Safe Zones

Many international conflicts relate to territory rights over the sea and its inhabitants. Take, for instance, the Bajau Laut and Orang Laut on the waters between Malaysia, Indonesia and the Phillipines. These people are originally nomadic boat dwellers, who create communities at sea by mooring a large number of boats together. In this way, family groups are created where the members regularly return to their floating home base at communal anchorage, between periods when they are away fishing. The communities have a constantly changing composition: people come and go continuously. For a long time, due to their nomadic existence at sea, these peoples had no nationality: Malaysia, Indonesia and the Phillipines were not interested in them and shifted responsibility

Sea nomads' houses on stilts at Semporna, Sabah, Borneo, Malaysia.

Stretching across part of
south-western Bangladesh
and south-eastern India, the
Sundarbans is the largest
remaining tract of mangrove
forest in the world. The
Sundarbans is a tapestry
of waterways, mudflats
and forested islands at the
edge of the Bay of Bengal.
The satellite image shows
the forest in the protected
area. The Sundarbans are
deep green, surrounded to
the north by a landscape of
agricultural lands, which are
lighter green, towns, which
are tan, and streams, which
are blue. This image was
created by merging Landsat
7 satellite observations
from 24 November 1999,
and 17 and 26 November
2000.

for these people onto each other. However, this type of entirely floating existence is becoming increasingly rare. It is a
way of life that no longer fits in modern society. Many families
now settle for part of the year in dwellings on stilts on the
water. They regularly alternate periods of seasonal work on
land with long stays at sea. The problem of their nationality is
automatically solved by their fixed place of residence.

Another boundary dispute that has been automatically
solved by the consequences of modern society is the years-long
argument between Bangladesh and India about a small island
in the Bay of Bengal, known to Indians as New Moore Island
and to Bangladeshis as South Talpatti Island. Recent satellite
images show that the island has in fact completely disappeared
under water, as a result of the rising sea level. 'What these two
countries could not achieve during years of talking, has been
resolved by global warming,' oceanographer Sugata Hazra of
Jadavpur University in Calcutta told the BBC in March 2010. In
its heyday, the island was never more than 2 m above sea level
and was uninhabited, but other islands in the Sunderban delta
region that are inhabited are expected to disappear under

water in the coming years as well, causing a large number of climate refugees. 'We will have ever larger numbers of people displaced from the Sunderbans as more island areas come under water,' said Hazra in the same interview.[28]

Financially weaker countries will be the big losers in an era of climate changes. While rich countries manage to raise record amounts for recovery and coastal defence after a tsunami, the same countries do not seem to be capable of providing a large-scale solution for the vulnerability of the delta dwellers in Bangladesh. Unlike in the Netherlands, where the low-lying country's safety is secured by high-tech dikes and defence systems, the Bangladesh delta is exposed and vulnerable to every rise in sea level. Furthermore, extreme rainfall combined with asphalt creates an increased risk of flooding in these regions.

Instead of waiting until the Western world once again comes up with solutions after a disaster has taken place, the population can join in battle against water in a more structural way. In order to find a suitable solution, a low-tech, low-cost floating platform made from local materials will have to be devised.

The inhabitants of Myanmar (Birma) do not have to look far for the answer. Something similar is already in use in agriculture by the people living near the Inle Lake in the Shan Hills. Locals grow vegetables and fruit in large gardens that float on the surface of the lake. The floating garden beds are formed by extensive manual labour. Farmers gather up lake-bottom weeds from the deeper parts of the lake, bring them back in boats and make them into floating beds in their garden areas, anchored by bamboo poles. These gardens rise and fall with changes in the water level, and so are resistant to flooding. The constant availability of nutrient-laden water results in these gardens being incredibly fertile.

Floating Gardens on Inle Lake, Shan State, Myanmar (Burma).

Approximately 20 km south of Cambodia's most important attraction – the temples of Angkor – lies the floating village of Chong Khneas in the Tonlé Sap Lake. The floating houses, petrol stations, little churches and pigpens start at the mouth of the river that flows from Siem Reap to the lake. Fishing is the most important source of income; the younger generation tries to earn a little on the side as 'guides' on the tourist boats that visit the area.

Green in the City

Floating landscapes can play an important role in the promotion of prosperity, not just in sparsely populated coastal regions, but also in heavily urbanized landscapes. The morphology of the city consists of a mixture of buildings, asphalted open areas, green spaces and water. Greenery has more than just a visual function in this respect. Parks are very important for air quality, ecological structure and social coherence. People looking for space for green facilities in large cities have tended to look at flat roofs up until now as a place to realize greenery. However, many cities have considerably more potential spots for green areas: on the water. By locating greenery on water, the quality of the city can improve. Floating parks, gardens and quays are dynamic and flexible, so they can

URBAN GREENERY IS NOT A POINTLESS DECORATION, IT IS A NECESSITY

provide freedom when designing and maintaining the city. They can be sailed in at the moment a neighbourhood is completed to give the new district an immediate mature character. If floating city districts are to be taken seriously, green spaces need to be integrated. Urban greenery is not a pointless decoration, it is a necessity.

INCREA

SING UF

BAN SU

STAINA

BILITY

aninconvenienttruth

A GLOBAL WARNING

www.climatecrisis.net

Chapter 7

SUSTAINA-QUALITY

Architects like to talk about sustainability. Ever since William McDonough and Michael Braungart published their book *Cradle to Cradle* in 2002 and Al Gore brought out the documentary *An Inconvenient Truth* in 2006, you are not worth your salt as an architect (or builder, developer or producer of building materials) if you are not involved in sustainable activities. Notwithstanding all the good intentions, the word has been subject to serious hyperbole in recent years. If you believe PR companies, almost everything is sustainable these days. For instance, the Ecobuild fair in London's Earls Court in March 2010 was full of exhibitors of building materials that claimed to be good for the environment, but finding genuinely environmentally friendly materials was like looking for a needle in a haystack.

Op 17 May 2009, thousands of people gathered on St Kilda Beach, Melbourne, for a Human Sign rally. Together they formed the words 'Climate change – our future is in your hands'. With this message the Australians wanted to make clear, a few days before the start of the Climate Conference in Copenhagen, that they were not satisfied with the limited attention their government was paying to climate change.

Not many people can provide a good explanation of what sustainability actually means. Is a building sustainable if it uses little energy? If it is constructed from building materials whose manufacture has cost little energy? If it has been built using locally available materials? If it has been built using materials that are as recyclable as possible? In spite of all the attempts to define, classify and standardize calculation methods, there is still a great deal of Babel-like confusion about sustainability because it is such a complicated subject.

It doesn't help either that the most recent climate conference, held in Copenhagen in December 2009, is generally considered as a failure. After the event, many countries and environmental organizations spoke of an utter fiasco, because no binding agreements were made about CO_2 reduction. Seen from a marketing viewpoint, the environment as a buzz word has to a certain extent become a victim of its own success. The subject has been an enormous hype the last few years, in part due to genuine concerns about the future of the planet or merely as an attempt to increase turnover. By now, the commercial and political interests are enormous. Perhaps that was the reason that during the conference some of the figures relating to climate predictions were revealed to be exaggerated. The climate sceptics seized on these errors to label the representatives of the Intergovernmental Panel on Climate Change as 'frauds' and 'climate mafia'.

The environment is too important to become the victim of fanatics at both ends of the spectrum. Since a number of European scientists founded the Club of Rome in 1968, most politicians take problems such as the explosive growth of the world population, inadequate food production, industrialization, exhaustion of natural resources and pollution seriously. The solution to these problems is a lengthy process and it is therefore important to carry out the environmental debate on the basis of correct information.

Demolishing buildings that are structurally still perfectly sound is not only destruction of capital but also generates a large amount of unnecessary demolition waste. Pictured on the photo is the controlled demolition of four buildings in one city block in Johannesburg to make way for a multistorey parking garage for the new Gautrain underground railway.

The Building Sector as Polluter

The building sector is a major contributor to environmental damage in many countries. In the Netherlands, for instance, the building sector is responsible for 6 per cent of the Gross Domestic Product, but for around 35 per cent of road transport and approximately 35 per cent of the mountain of waste. Furthermore, around 50 per cent of resources are intended directly or indirectly for the building sector and the developed environment is responsible for about 40 per cent of CO_2 emissions. As a result, the building industry plays an important role in the environmental debate.[29]

The most practical and in all likelihood ultimately the most effective form of sustainability is flexibility. A building is sustainable if it has a very long life and a building has a long life if it is flexible. The Tower of London, for example, was sustainable long before the word was invented. In the course

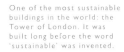

One of the most sustainable buildings in the world: the Tower of London. It was built long before the word 'sustainable' was invented.

of the centuries, the building has served as fort, royal palace, state prison, mint, garrison, museum and arsenal. It was able to fulfil so many functions because it combines a solid supporting structure with large interior spaces that can be used in various different ways. In spite of its massive appearance, it is a flexible building. Architects and developers who wish to build durably can still learn a great deal from this type of building.

From Sustainability to Sustainaquality

The pursuit of sustainability usually focuses on recycling building materials, improving the return on heating and cooling systems and the use of alternative, green sources of energy. All of these are important and worthwhile aims but one major way of achieving sustainability is often overlooked: buildings that do not have to be demolished before the end of their life, technically speaking, yield the most obvious environmental savings, which additionally make many other sorts of economies pale into insignificance. The pursuit of sustainability should therefore be focused primarily on extending the useful life of the building. A longer period of usage means less new building production.

Water can also play an important role in the debate about sustainability. Sustainaquality is the search for new and effective ways to increase the sustainability of buildings and other urban components by using water.

Water can play a role in five different ways. You can make buildings flexible by making them buoyant and extending their economic lifespan as a result; you can improve the quality of water with floating elements; you can use the wind speed over water for ventilation and you can use the thermal capacity of water to cool and heat buildings. And last but not least: you can generate energy with water; the possibilities in this area have already been discussed in chapter 3.

Flexible Buildings

Floating buildings are easy to move if they are no longer required. They can begin a new life at a different location. In this way, they can have a much longer life. In most countries, buildings are regularly demolished long before the end of their technically achievable lifespan, because of the way the country's economic systems are organized. The economic lifespan of buildings is usually shorter than their technical lifespan. If the value of the land they are situated on also increases, it is not difficult to do the arithmetic in many cases: demolish the thing and replace it with a building containing more square metres.

Consequently, buildings that are technically in perfect condition are

On the right-hand side, the now-demolished Black Madonna apartment complex in The Hague. The neorationalist building with 336 apartments was designed by Dutch architect Carel Weeber and completed in 1985. In 2007, the complex was demolished, although it was still in very good structural condition. It had to make room for new-build designed for the Ministries of Justice and Home Affairs by German architect Hans Kollhoff.

regularly demolished without so much as a by your leave. For example, this is what happened to the Black Madonna apartment complex in The Hague, designed by architect Carel Weeber. The much-loved home to 336 families was built in 1985 but demolished in 2007 because the ground it was built on had risen so much in value that it was more profitable to replace it with a much larger building. The German architect Hans Kollhoff designed two high towers for the ministries of Home Affairs and Justice at this location. From a financial point of view, this was perfectly justifiable, unfortunately, but seen from an environmental standpoint and taking architecture history into account, it was a minor disaster.

This sort of problem does not arise with floating buildings. If a building is no longer required at a particular

SUSTAINAQUALITY IS THE SEARCH FOR NEW WAYS TO INCREASE SUSTAINABILITY BY USING WATER

location, you sell it and the new owner can moor it somewhere else. Just like a houseboat. There is no waste, no squandering of materials and energy. That makes urban design not just more environmentally friendly, but also more flexible. It is like a game of chess: you move your pieces to the squares where they are most needed, or where they are most useful.

Naturally, critics complain that floating buildings generally do not have foundations made from green materials. However, floating buildings make sustainability possible without having to utilize materials seen as environmentally friendly in everyday terms. As long as the materials have a long life, that is what counts. The current generation of foundations for floating buildings are made of concrete with perhaps the addition of polystyrene for buoyancy. These materials are not exactly known as environmentally friendly. A great deal of energy is required to produce polystyrene, and benzene and styrene are released during the process. Concrete consists of sand, coarse aggregate and cement. The cement in particular has consequences for the environment: like polystyrene, it takes a lot of energy to produce due to the sintering process and the grinding to a powder. Furthermore, concrete contains steel reinforcement. Its production costs a lot of energy and a lot of waste products are released as well.

But once concrete and steel have taken on their ultimate shape, they last a very long time. A floating foundation slab stays in good condition for at least a hundred years; that is four times as long as the 25 years used these days to write off office and industrial buildings, for example. Concrete buildings are generally demolished because they are no longer required, not because the concrete no longer comes up to scratch. That is not necessary with floating buildings, because they can be relocated and their lifespan is therefore considerably longer than that of fixed buildings. In addition, floating concrete foundations are prefabricated under well-controlled conditions. In the factory, the production process can be much better managed than for concrete that is processed on site, which improves the quality and reduces waste. Furthermore, concrete can be recycled in the form of granules after it has finally fulfilled its complete technical lifespan.

Improvement in the Quality of Water

Another environmental argument that is sometimes used as a criticism of floating buildings is that they throw a shadow on the bottom of the water in which they are situated and that they are not beneficial to the living organisms in the water as a result. This criticism seems credible at first sight. Large platforms undeniably exclude sunlight and that can be a disadvantage in cold climates in some locations, such as areas of natural beauty. In urban areas, however, the positive effects associated with floating platforms have the upper hand. Water in cities such as canals, channelled rivers and harbours are characterized by a firm division between land and water. Quaysides are practically all made of stone and the water beds have often been dredged, so there is hardly any differentiation in water depth and vegetation on the banks. As a result, the water environment is uniform and provides little protection for fish or other aquatic life. Floating platforms give the water environment an extra dimension.

In addition, in warm regions the heat-resistant properties of floating platforms are in fact most welcome. After all, they lead to a localized lower water temperature and that stimulates diversity in water milieus. The platforms also provide a protected habitats for small fish and other aquatic animals.

Platforms moored in warm waters provide cooling shadow under water, which has a positive effect on diversity in the water environment. Water plants and shellfish can cling to the underside of the platform.

A good example of a habitat underneath a buoyant construction is the hanging mussel culture. With this method, mussels grow on strands suspended in the water under work rafts and hanging culture racks. This is a popular method of cultivating mussels that was copied from a much older, undesirable phenomenon. The growth of mussels on the hulls of ships under the water line has been a significant problem since time immemorial. A layer of algae and shellfish quickly forms, especially in tropical waters, and this increases the hull's resistance, affecting performance. In the cold waters of Northern Europe, a layer like this grows to a 'beard' of some 10 cm long in a year. Even one hundredth of a millimetre of 'fouling' spread over a large surface increases a ship's fuel consumption by 1 per cent. Without the use of anti-fouling agents, the fuel consumption of oil tankers increases dramatically in a short space of time. Floating platforms do not suffer from this problem, of course. After all, they hardly need to move at all; only on the very occasional moments that they need to be relocated.

The underside of floating platforms can even be rough, porous or uneven, to encourage the attachment and growth of water plants, algae and shellfish. The water plants have a purifying effect on the water. The roots hanging in the water attract nutrients and absorb pollution. In this way the water is kept naturally clean, which gives algae less of a chance.

In tropical regions, floating islands can play a role in improving water quality and the habitat for fish in a sustainable way. In the Maldives, for example, pieces of coral have been damaged by the effect of sunlight. This phenomenon is called coral bleaching.

On 17 October 2009, president Mohamed Nasheed of the Maldives and members of his cabinet met underwater to stress the significance of rising seas in a world that is warming up (See chapter 6). The Associated Press reported: 'As bubbles floated up from their face masks, the president, vice president, Cabinet secretary and 11 ministers signed a document calling on all countries to cut their carbon dioxide emissions.'

It is a condition that can cause serious damage and entire coral reefs can die off as a result. Coral contains microscopic algae, which provide the coral with food and give it a striking colour. If the water temperature rises, the coral is affected by stress, which makes it keep out the algae. The consequence is bleaching. If this process continues, it ultimately leads to the death of the coral. A rise of only 1° C above the maximum temperature in the summer can be enough to cause the coral to bleach. The average temperature in tropical seas has risen by 1° C in the last century, and many people expect this rise to continue.

Coral bleaching is a consequence of increased water temperature or increased solar irradiance. The consequence is that entire reefs turn pale and ultimately die. Once they have died, they are lost forever. Floating platforms can provide protection against coral bleaching, because they can supply shade and coolness in seas that are warming up.

The problem is also present in the world-famous Great Barrier Reef, which lies off the coast of Queensland

in Australia. It is the largest reef in the world with a length of 2,000 km. The most serious case of coral bleaching took place in 2002, when more than 60 per cent of the reef was damaged. Unless the expected climate changes are delayed, a large part of the reef will be dead in a few decades. Biologists expect the hundreds of animal species dependent on the reef to die as well, if they are robbed of their natural environment. In-depth studies have not yet been carried out, but perhaps floating beaches above the coral could have a positive effect on coral growth.

Air Cooling

Building on water provides opportunities to bring sustainable building to a new level in many other ways. In chapter 6, the concept of heat stress was mentioned. Urban Heat Islands are cities that are significantly warmer than the surrounding countryside. The phenomenon has been known about for a very long time. The first person to describe it, although he did not yet give it this name, was Luke Howard, who published a two-part book in 1818 and 1820 with the title *The climate of London, deduced from Meteorological observations, made at different places in the neighbourhood of the metropolis.* Apart from the parks described in the previous chapter, urban ventilation is also essential for the health and comfort of city dwellers. Natural ventilation is less effective in urban surroundings than in open areas, partly due to the higher density of the building blocks and the phenomenon of Urban Heat Islands.

In spite of the fact that Urban Heat Islands have been recognized for a long time, urban cooling is a topic that has not been studied very much. Pioneers in this field are Khaled Al-Sallal and Rashed Al Al-Shaali of the United Arab Emirates University. They are using computer models to investigate various urban configurations and their possibilities for passive cooling, which should lead to well-ventilated cities with a high level of thermal comfort. The scientists have discovered that buildings limit good air flow in many cities, particularly when the prevailing wind speed is less than 3 m/s. In these situations, an oppressive, unpleasant city climate is created. There is sufficient thermal comfort from approximately 5 m/s, but these wind speeds cause unacceptable whirlwinds at the

THE

CLIMATE OF LONDON,

DEDUCED FROM

Meteorological Observations,

MADE AT DIFFERENT PLACES

IN THE

NEIGHBOURHOOD OF THE METROPOLIS.

By LUKE HOWARD.

IN TWO VOLUMES.

VOL. II.

Containing (besides a Preface to the second volume) the remainder of the Series of Observations, up to Midsummer 1819 : an Account of the Climate, under the heads of *Temperature*, Barometrical *Pressure*, *Winds*, *Evaporation*, *Moisture* by the Hygrometer, *Rain*, *Lunar periods* : with a *Summary* of Results, in the order of the seasons ; *General Tables* ; and a copious *Index*.

LONDON:

PRINTED AND SOLD BY W. PHILLIPS, GEORGE YARD, LOMBARD STREET : SOLD ALSO BY J. AND A. ARCH, CORNHILL ; BALDWIN, CRADOCK, AND JOY, AND W. BENT, PATERNOSTER ROW ; AND J. HATCHARD, PICCADILLY.

1820.

Title page of *The climate of London, deduced from Meteorological observations, made at different places in the neighbourhood of the metropolis.* The study was written by Luke Howard, and published in two parts in 1818 and 1820.

corners of buildings. In warm, dry climates, the trick is to design the street patterns and the shape of the buildings in such a way that there is sufficient ventilation without causing eddies. In floating cities, the effect of an optimal configuration of the building blocks is logically greater than on land, because wind speeds on water are higher than on shore.

Good natural ventilation can result in a comfortable and healthy interior environment and also provide energy savings. Natural ventilation and thermal comfort are often difficult for developers to understand. It is important for urban designers, architects and engineers to consult early on in the design process with experts in the field of urban ventilation about the geometric structure of the urban environment. In this way, sustainable master planning can lead to an optimal result.

FLOATING ISLANDS CAN IMPROVE WATER QUALITY AND THE HABITAT FOR FISH IN A SUSTAINABLE WAY

Water Cooling

Water can also serve to temper extremes in heat and cold in a more direct way. These days, a large number of buildings are equipped with a heat pump. In the winter, warm groundwater is additionally pumped up from a depth of dozens of metres, which can be used to heat a building. After the water has given off its warmth, it goes back into the ground as cold water, where it is stored. In the summer, the water can be brought above ground again, but this time used to cool the building. After the water has absorbed the heat from the building, it is once again stored underground, to be used again the following winter for heating purposes. And so it goes on.

This is an environmentally friendly heating system that is being used more and more often, but is also expensive to install. Why pump water from the depths of the earth when open water has exactly the same characteristics? Large masses of water such as lakes and seas shift temperature more slowly than earth mass. That is why the sea feels cold in the spring, and only really warms up towards the end of the summer. For the same reason, a sea climate is more temperate than a continental climate. If you take that fact into account, it is possible to incorporate the use of water for heating and cooling purposes into the design of floating buildings. By pumping water through the building, the internal temperature can be lowered in the summer and raised in the winter.

Floating Mosque

A world without air conditioning in prosperous tropical societies is almost unimaginable these days. Cooled air is essential to create a liveable indoor climate in hot countries. However, air conditioners are energy guzzlers. For that reason, it can do no harm to see of it can be done differently on water.

Waterstudio has come up with a practical application using the possibilities water offers for heat and cold storage in their design for a floating mosque in the Arabian Gulf, off the coast of Dubai. The thermal capacity of water works in the same way as that of stone. If you go into a church on a hot summer's day, the cool temperature inside is often like a breath of fresh air. The church probably does not have air conditioning; what you experience is the radiation of coolness that has been stored in the thick stone walls at night. Heat or cold storage needs mass and that is exactly what the walls of old churches can provide. This type of heat and cold storage can take place not just in stone, but also in water.

Large seas have a fairly constant temperature. Water represents a large mass with an enormous heat or cold capacity. In cold climates, water can operate as a source of cooling. In the summer the cold that was stored in the water during the winter can be radiated.

In order to use water to cool a building, there has to be a difference between the indoor temperature and the temperature of the water. This temperature differential has to be transferred from one medium (water) to the other

Design by Waterstudio for a floating mosque off the coast of Dubai. Although the design proposal is innovative, all the traditional elements of a mosque are present. Two minarets make it possible to call the faithful to prayer five times a day. A footbath is provided in the forecourt for ritual cleansing before prayers. The five columns, through which sea water is pumped, represent the Five Pillars of Islam: the profession of faith, ritual prayers, fasting during Ramadan, giving of alms and the pilgrimage to Mecca.

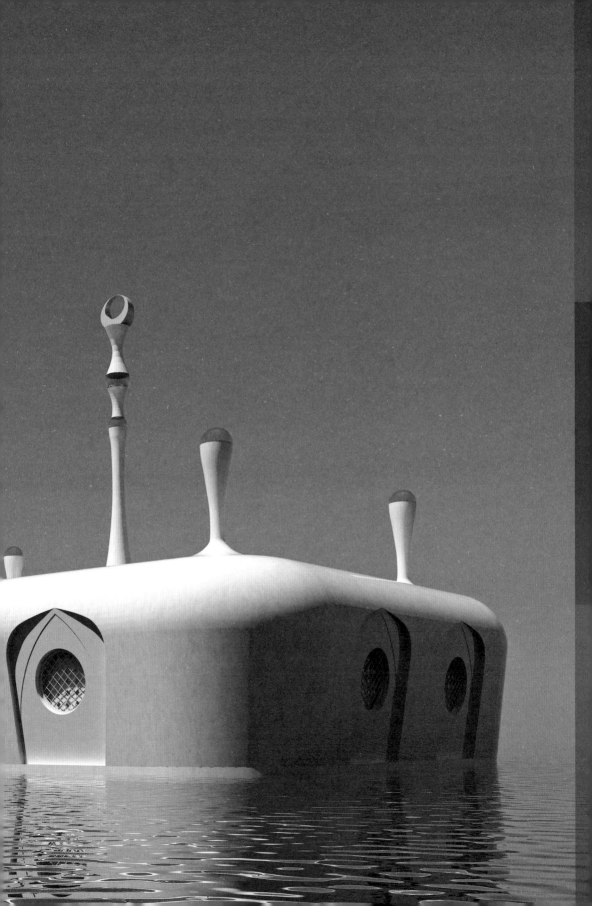

Design by Waterstudio for
a floating mosque off the
coast of Dubai.

medium (interior atmosphere). There are two ways to achieve
this. The first is a closed system where a cooling liquid takes
on the temperature of the water on the outside and gives off
this cold to the walls and floors of the interior space. Floor
heating in a house works in the same way but then in reverse:
in this case, heat is transferred instead of cold. The other
possibility is an open system, where cold water is transported
directly through the walls without the intervention of a transfer liquid. This open system is used for the climate installation
in the design for the Floating Mosque.

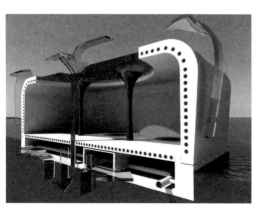

The clients requested the use
of a sustainable cooling system instead
of air conditioning, partly because the
mosque was to be situated on open
water, without a direct connection to
the quayside. As a result, energy transport from the quay to the mosque is
not possible; all the energy will need
to be generated in the mosque itself. In
traditional designs, diesel generators are
often used for this purpose.

The requirement was set for the mosque to be as self-sufficient as possible. The solution lies in three principles. Firstly, the roof and walls absorb little heat because they have a porous external cladding, consisting of a sponge-like ceramic material that functions according to the same principle as the underside of the Space Shuttle: the material heats up and cools down quickly, because it cannot retain any heat due to its extremely low density. A somewhat more vulnerable outside is not a problem, because the mosque is situated on water. Secondly, open-system water cooling allows sea water to be pumped at high speed through the walls, roof and floor, for optimal uptake of warmth. Finally, the thick external walls have a high accumulative capacity, due to their high density and large size.

Its openness means that the chance of pollution is greater than in closed systems. To combat this, a choice has been made to use a flow tube with an extra large diameter. The diameter is 120 mm: similar to a substantial rainwater drainpipe. Filter tanks also ensure that the water is first filtered before it is sent through the walls of the mosque.

In the prayer hall, the glass roof is supported by five columns representing the pillars of Islam. Roof and columns have been made transparent by using composed acrylic pieces. This material is normally used for large sea aquariums. Sea water is led from outside via the filter through the floor and walls to the roof, after which it leaves the building again over the glass roof via the columns. A transport regulator ensures that the columns are always sufficiently full, to give them a visually attractive appearance.

The outside temperature can rise in the summer in the UAE to 50° C. The sea water warms up to a maximum of 27° C. The water cooling and cold accumulation ultimately give the inside walls a temperature of 30° C. The inside air temperature takes over the temperature of the internal walls almost completely, by convection and radiation. Solar-driven air conditioning brings the temperature down even further to 21°C. Solar energy is also required for the pumping installation.

Water cooling at sea has no effect on the heating management of the sea, in contrast with water cooling in a small lake or canal. The sea is an inexhaustible mass with a constant temperature. Sustainaquality makes use of this cool mass to create higher sustainability. Large-scale use of water

cooling at sea provides many future possibilities for floating urban design.

Scarless Developments

Urban living environments leave scars behind in the landscape. In the same way that metabolism cannot take place without damaging and ageing the human body, the use of space is also an assault on the natural surroundings. It begins even before a single brick has been laid. Before building can take place in peaty regions, a layer of several metres of sand first has to be dumped in the landscape. This sand layer must lie for at least a year, and usually longer, so that the peat can settle under the weight of the parcel of sand. Subsequently, piles are driven into the sub layer to keep the foundations straight. Infrastructure and utilities also damage the pristine condition of the original landscape. And then the huge land reclamation projects that take place worldwide, during which large amounts of sand are dumped to create land, have not even been mentioned yet. Permanent damage to the original landscape is the result.

These large-scale harmful effects are a characteristic of modern society. Before the industrial revolution in the nineteenth century made large-scale landscape interventions possible, the influence of human activity on the natural environment was relatively limited. Even the creation of polders in

the Netherlands took place with limited means. In addition, long ago a relatively large number of people led a nomadic existence. The nomadic peoples on the steppes of Mongolia and the desert folk in the Middle East migrated from region to region without leaving any traces of their stay. Similarly, primitive people like the Aboriginals in Australia, the Bushmen in New Guinea and the Eskimos at the North Pole used the space available to them without causing any damage.

In the discussion about sustainable building, attention should also be paid to the temporary use of space without causing any lasting damage. After all, we borrow space from nature. 'Scarless development' is building without damaging the landscape. In this case, it is not just about the building work carried out but the use of the space as well. In the ideal situation, a building has no carbon footprint during its lifespan and leaves no physical footprint behind afterwards.

... traditional New Guinea huts in an Indonesian mountain village ...

... and an Igloo in a winter mountain setting.

Carbon-Free Footprint

Various countries are undertaking serious attempts to build carbon-free cities. The best-known example is Mazdar City in Abu Dhabi. However, even this city will leave a physical footprint behind. The Cradle to Cradle ideology certainly helped in the search for ways to reuse materials, but it does not mention the physical footprint buildings inflict on their location.

(Left)
This is not an example of scarless development: the hundreds of piles necessary for building foundations in soft or wet ground create a permanent footprint at the construction location.

(Right)
Enormous amounts of sand are required to create new landfill in Dubai, UAE. The sand often comes from pristine beaches on tropical islands. Sand extraction irreparably damages nature there.

Palm Island in Dubai, UAE.

In this respect, floating buildings represent the least intrusive structures for a landscape. Their foundations leave no traces in the substructure, and the installation of utilities, roads and other infrastructure has no negative effects on the ground, either. Once a floating building has left its location, there will be nothing left to remind people of its former presence. In this respect, the floating city is a little reminiscent of the wonderful Bacardi advertisement 'Island' made in 2009, which was filmed off the coast of Malta. In the ad, a large number of partygoers congregate on boats and make a temporary island with rocks, sand and palm trees. The following morning, there is nothing to remind people of the enchanted night before, other than a disco ball floating in the pristine water. In this way, advertising agency Young & Rubicam link the alcoholic drink not just to values such as optimism, imagination and a pioneering spirit, but even manage to reference, in an impressive way, a lifestyle that leaves hardly any negative footprint on its surroundings, in spite of its extravagant, mobile character.

Although in the advert part of the party takes place on the boats that have joined the spectacle, the heart is

formed by a temporary landfill of stones in the water. In fact, that was not really necessary; the ad would have been even better if a floating island had been given this role. After all, that has no footprint whatsoever.

Floating versus Landfill

The continually growing space requirements experienced by cities on the water is one of the driving forces behind the dredging industry. Naturally, this solution is not very sustainable. New land is created by introducing a sand mass in the water, but the underwater milieu disappears. In addition, the influence of new land on natural water currents causes problems.

For example, that was what the UAE discovered when they constructed the Palm Jumeirah. As long ago as 2003, when the island was only half-completed, it became clear that the surrounding beaches were being affected by the altered sea current. The Rotterdam dredging company Van Oord, responsible for constructing Palm Jumeirah, had to turn out to raise the height of the beaches and place an extra breakwater here and there, to keep the existing coastline intact.

The situation was dangerous, particularly in places where buildings were positioned directly on the coast, because the foundations could be damaged.

Palm Jumeirah has itself experienced problems too, particularly in the areas of water quality and temperature. The water keeps getting saltier and the water temperature is already around 35° C in the summer. 'If the water between the fronds of the Palm stays still, it is not unthinkable that it will reach 40 degrees. That feels like boiling hot,' said urban designer Han Meyer in 2005 in Delft University of Technology's weekly magazine *Delta*.[30]

Another disadvantage of landfill is that the filled-in island needs a long period to settle and become robust enough for new building works. This waiting time can rise to a few years in some cases, depending on the thickness of the layer of sand.

However, the biggest problem with landfill islands is that not only the new location is affected, but also the place the sand came from. The amounts of sand needed for land reclamation projects are gigantic. Dredger Van Oord, for example, required 125 million m³ of sand and 13 million tons of stone for The World in Dubai island group. Sand for The World was taken from nearby offshore extraction areas, in the same way as for the other islands, using trailing suction hopper dredgers. These ranged in capacity from 2,300 m³ to 23,000 m³. The stones were brought in with large barges and positioned by stone dumpers and split barges. Sand is becoming increasingly scarce, due to the enormous demand in some parts of the world.

Sometimes sand extraction can even lead to conflicts. In 2002 there was a 'sand war' between Singapore on one

An island in The World, Dubai, UAE.

side and Malaysia and Indonesia on the other. The dredging companies were getting their supplies of sand from Malaysia and Indonesia for three enormous land reclamation projects off the coast of Singapore, but after a disagreement between the countries, deliveries to Singapore were halted and therefore also the dredging projects. According to Malaysia, the narrowing of the strait near Singapore would endanger shipping

and the environment would be damaged, while Indonesia accused Singapore of illegal dredging activities. [31]

Years later, the argument had not yet been resolved. In fact, after Cambodia and Vietnam also prohibited the export of sand to Singapore, *The Telegraph* reported in February 2010 that Singapore was accused of paying thieves to steal entire beaches under cover of night: 'The thieves have begun making night-time raids on the picturesque sandy beaches of Indonesia and Malaysia, carving out millions of tons of coastline and leading to fears of an imminent environmental catastrophe on a swath of tropical islands... Singapore's land developers are now pitted against environmental groups, who claim several of the 83 border islands off the north coast of Indonesia could disappear into the sea in the next decade unless the smugglers are stopped.'

When Greenpeace got wind of the situation, they became involved as well. 'It is a war for natural resources that is being fought secretly,' said Nur Hidayati, Greenpeace's spokesman in Indonesia, in the British newspaper. 'The situation has reached critical levels and the tropical islands of Nipah, the Karimun islands and many small islands off the coast of Riau are shrinking dramatically and on the brink of disappearing into the sea. The whole marine ecosystem in the areas where uncontrolled sand extraction is taking place is being destroyed – tropical fish species

Example of scarless development: a Waterstudio design for a floating house with floating gardens off the coast of Dubai.

and barrier reefs are dying and the region's marine biodiversity is under threat.' To crown it all, *The Telegraph* also reported that '34 Malaysian civil servants were arrested for accepting bribes and sexual favours to facilitate the sand smuggling to Singapore'. It is estimated that every year approximately 300 m^3 of sand are exported illegally from Indonesia in this way. [32]

Floating islands have none of these disadvantages. No waiting time for settling, no damage to vulnerable eco-systems in other parts of the world, only a slight influence on water currents and no destruction of the underwater environment. Compared to traditional land reclamation projects, floating islands actually contribute to sustainaquality.

Sustainability is an innovation process where new and more effective methods need to interact in a durable

'SCARLESS DEVELOP-MENT' IS BUILDING WITHOUT DAMAGING THE LANDSCAPE

way with the surroundings. Scarless development will need to become the standard for buildings and cities in the future. Water can provide a whole range of solutions but most of them have only just been discovered and put into practice. Sustainaquality can play an important role in the pursuit of sustainability: it is already bobbing up and down, just waiting to be picked up by the climate change generation.

REGULA

ATING EX

XPANSIC

ON ONT

O WATE

The self-proclaimed micronation Sealand is established on a former marine platform in the North Sea.

Chapter 8

SEA OF OPPORTUNITIES

On 2 September 1967, former British soldier Roy Bates raised the flag he designed himself on the remains of Fort Roughs, just outside British territorial waters in the North Sea. He declared the independence of his new mini-state, called it Sealand and appointed himself the Prince of Sealand. The fresh new prince had already had several previous careers at that moment. He had first served as a major in the British Army and later been a fisherman and radio pirate. When he took over Radio City in 1965, he had occupied the Knock John Tower, like Fort Roughs part of the Maunsell Sea Forts already mentioned in chapter 3. He had first renamed the station Radio Essex and subsequently rechristened it Britain's Better Music Station (BBMS) in October 1966.

After only a few months, the British government ordered
him to stop the broadcasts. However, Bates did not give in
and took over the 550-m² Roughs Tower. That had already
been claimed by Jack Moore and his daughter for Ronan
O'Rahilly from Radio Caroline, so it led to a few small scuffles. The story goes that Bates was able to stand his ground,
however, by firing small bombs at the boat holding O'Rahilly's
men, among other actions. The planned radio station never
came into being, but he decided to stay on the island anyway,
together with his wife. After a while, the couple packed it in
again; Bates, who was born in 1922, is now retired and living
in Spain. His son Michael, who was discharged from the
British Army as a result of his father's actions, goes through
life as the Prince Regent of Sealand.[33]

Bates was not the only person who wanted to use
the relative lawlessness of the open sea to establish his own
nation, and thus avoid paying taxes. History is full of such free
spirits. In the same year Bates proclaimed his independent
state, Italian engineer Giorgio Rosa financed the construction
of a 400-m² platform in the Adriatic Sea, 7 miles off the coast
of Rimini, Italy. He equipped the platform with amenities such
as a restaurant, a bar, a nightclub, a souvenir shop and a post
office. On 24 June 1968, the time had come: he declared the

Rose Island was a micronation on a drilling platform at the end of the 1960s. It was situated in the Adriatic Sea, off the Italian coast near Rimini. The official language was Esperanto. Photo from a page in *Panorama*, 11 July 1968.

CCIAIO E CALCESTRUZZO. A 11 chilometri e 600 metri al
ırgo di Rimini (al difuori delle acque territoriali) sorge la
iattaforma voluta dall'ingegner Giorgio Rosa. Poggia su 9 pila-

stri d'acciaio riempiti di calcestruzzo e ha una superficie
di 400 metri quadrati. Attualmente sull'isola vive soltanto
Bernardini che l'ha affittata per un anno.

platform independent and named it Rose Island.[34] His monarchist aspirations were less pronounced than Bates's; he modestly appointed himself President. However, Rose Island did not last long either. The Italian government saw Rosa's enterprise mainly as an attempt to avoid taxes and had the Marines blow up the platform with explosives, after a group of four carabinieri and tax inspectors had impounded it.[35]

It is easy to dismiss Bates, Rosa and their kindred spirits as oddballs trying to wriggle out from under the apparently oppressive laws of their native countries. But they are not alone. Besides individuals, entire organizations try to use the freedom of the seas to establish autonomous communities that fall outside the legislation of existing countries. The aim of the Seasteading Institute, for instance, initiated by Wayne Gramlich and Patri Friedman on 15 April 2008, is to build mobile communities in international waters. The project received a lot of media attention (from CNN and *Wired Magazine*, among others) after PayPal founder Peter Thiel invested half a million dollars in the institute in 2008 and expressed a positive opinion about the project's feasibility. 'When Seasteading becomes a viable alternative, switching from one government to another would be a matter of sailing to the other without even leaving your house,' said Friedman during the first Seasteading conference in October of the same year.

In 2009 the institute organized a design prize. Contest entrants were provided with a 3-D model of the institute's

patented base platform, similar to an oil platform, on which
they were to build creative architectural designs for a new society of ocean pioneers. The specifics of the design, aesthet-
ics and intended use were entirely up to each designer. The
results certainly appeal to the imagination, but do not disguise
the fact that the aim of the Seasteading Institute is primarily
political: the establishment of an autonomous community that
does not fall under the jurisdiction of an existing country.[36]

In their quest for independence, these types of in-
triguing enterprises reveal an important fact: legislation is
not absolute. The laws on water are different from those on
land. If you build on water, you come up against issues need-
ing clarification and conflicting interests. Much is possible in

Overall winner of the Seasteading Institute design competition: The Swimming City by András Győrfi.

this vacuum, but existing countries and legal entities naturally defend their interests to the hilt, as the examples above illustrate. These uncertainties ultimately lead to new regulations. But until these new rules are in place, the strangest things are imaginable.

Discrepancies between Legislation and Practice

Laws are laid down at a particular moment in time, with a specific aim in mind. However, techniques and customs change, and that can reduce the relevance of legislation. As a consequence, possibilities can arise that were not previously foreseen. With the arrival of new buoyancy technologies it is now possible to colonize on water. Living on a floating underlayer is no longer utopia; it is common practice in many countries. The regulations relating to rights on water were, however, drawn up in another era, when technological, political and economic circumstances were different from today. The discrepancies between legislation and practice that come into existence as a result are sometimes deliberately misused.

In the current judicial system, there are laws for ships and other laws for houses. Ships lie in water, are moveable objects and can be relocated. Houses are situated on land, are fixed objects and are bound to their location. At first sight, this legal status makes a clear distinction between both sorts of construction. But what will happen if construction types emerge that fall between the two categories?

The first houseboats were barges that no longer moved. Due to inconveniences of maintenance, this type of boat was often kitted out with a concrete trough as buoyant construction. That made the structure more rectangular as well. In the 1990s, the public at large discovered the pleasures of living on the water. It was usually rich people who transformed houseboats into floating water houses. They were larger and more luxurious than traditional houseboats, sometimes with two or three storeys, but they continued to fall under the advantageous tax regulations applying to barges. The rules were never drawn up with these water palaces in mind. These days, there is still a great deal possible on water: floating islands, floating agriculture and moveable districts. The discrepancies between legislation and practice continue to grow as a result.

Some people take advantage of these discrepancies to avoid a demand for property taxes. When the Dutch municipality of Almere sent a tax demand to the inhabitant of a substantial water house moored to piles, the resident lodged an objection. After all, he lived on a ship, didn't he? After a court case

case failed to deliver the desired outcome, he took his case to the appeals court in Arnhem. In October 2007 the court judged that it indeed was a fixed object, but the owner was still not satisfied and took his case to the Supreme Court. To his delight, they overturned the court's ruling in January 2010, with the motivation that 'it is evident from its construction that the object in question is intended to float and does float, so it does concern a ship.' The motivation continued as follows: 'A ship is generally speaking a moveable object. A connection between a ship and the ground situated under that ship, which allows the ship to move in line with the water level, cannot lead to the conclusion that the ship is united with the ground.'[37]

It later transpired that the Dutch Ministry of Housing, Spatial Planning and the Environment viewed the case very

THE LAWS ON WATER ARE DIFFERENT FROM THOSE ON LAND

differently. In a letter to the Dutch Lower House on 26 November 2009, Minister Jacqueline Cramer had already written that 'it is credible that water houses that are not intended to sail after mooring and additionally, where the residents intend the houses to remain long-term at their location, are fixed objects.' Even after the judgement of the Supreme Court, the Minister stuck to her point of view, because the judge in question was apparently a fiscal judge and the verdict had mainly to do with tax affairs.[38]

Daily practice seems to agree with her: the municipality of Rotterdam even designated the SS Rotterdam, the former flagship of the Holland America Line, as a fixed object,

The retired ocean liner SS Rotterdam is permanently moored at a quay in Rotterdam harbour and is officially a fixed object.

after it had been transformed into a hotel and conference centre and permanently moored to spud poles in the Maas Harbour since 30 January 2009. Similarly, the Floating Pavilion designed by engineering firm DeltaSync, Public Domain Architects and Bart van Bueren, which was moored in the Rhine Harbour on 21 May 2010 and will serve for five years as an exhibition space about Rotterdam's climate programme, was designated a fixed object.

These sorts of discussions take place regularly on land too, for instance about the interpretation of rules for caravans. In many countries, caravans do not fall under the same sorts of rules as houses; after all, they are moveable objects. In the meantime, many caravans have expanded to become colossal villas, where you would really have to look closely to find barely functional wheels underneath, but legally speaking they are still caravans and the owners do not have to pay any tax. As long as the regulations remain unchanged, these owners are operating within the boundaries of the law.

Another fixed object: the Floating Pavilion in Rotterdam, designed by DeltaSync, Public Domain Architects and Bart van Bueren.

A Comparison with the Energy and Telecom Sectors

Whenever new products and services are developed in a society, and when two previously separate worlds come together as a result, it is often still unclear who is responsible for what and which rules apply. That not only creates legal and financial risks, but also huge opportunities for experimentation and innovation. This type of development was experienced by the energy and telecom sectors in the last decade. Around the year 2000, companies in these sectors presented their own products separately: telephone companies made sure people could make calls, other companies laid cables for

The Floating Pavilion will serve as an exhibitions space.

television and radio, and electricity was supplied by the municipal electricity company.

Liberalization of the energy and telecom markets, imposed on the member states by the European Union, led to the current situation where consumers in Europe can choose which energy supplier they use and who provides them with telecom services. In addition, the boundary between telephone, television and Internet is fading rapidly in the wake of technological developments. As a result, the differences between the various providers are also fading. At the moment, phoning via Skype is the cheapest method and many young people spend more time on YouTube these days than in front of the television, with the corresponding consequences for the required capacity of the network.

When these developments were still in their infancy about ten years ago, rules of play for the new market still had to be established. That did not progress without a struggle, and various companies wasted huge sums of money by assessing the situation incorrectly. In 2000, for instance, the Dutch government auctioned off UMTS frequencies. That had never happened before, but the public sale was deemed necessary in order to develop the market for mobile telephone communication. The sale of five UMTS frequencies yielded almost 2 billion euro for the Dutch government, but within a year some of the licence buyers were in financial difficulties because they had apparently paid too much. Unfamiliarity with the novelty of a UMTS public sale and uncertainty about the value of new services were the primary causes here. As a consequence, a second auction of mobile frequencies organized by the Dutch government in April 2010 realized far less than the sale a decade earlier. Similar scenarios took place in other European countries.

New communication technologies also provide a challenge in the field of legislation. Social networks such as Google Buzz, Facebook and Twitter are regularly in the news because they get their fingers smacked by watchdogs involved in the protection of personal data. The sites are accused of violating the privacy of their users, by trading personal information without explicit permission or by exposing the information in public. The relative newness of these types of social networks means that there is not yet specific legislation in this area. While there is no legislation, companies offering these services can continually overstep the mark without there being any judicial possibilities to combat the excesses. After all, when different services merge and new services come into existence, it is no longer clear which rules apply. It is up to the legislator to react to these social changes. The same is true of building on water.

With the arrival of new technologies it is now possible to colonize on water. The key question is: Do the regulations on water or on land apply here? Or is a new category of laws necessary, which not only distinguish between fixed and moveable objects but also recognize a third form? Or should the distinction between ground above and below the water be completely removed? The answers to these questions depend on the way in which building on water is given shape. Is it a question of the expansion of existing land or does it concern independent floating objects? Is the aim of the floating objects to move goods or people, or provide them with accommodation? Are the floating objects equipped with a drive mechanism or not?

There are already many more communities living on water than most people realize. On the North Sea alone, there are around 10,000 oil and gas platforms, of which a significant number are no longer operational. There are around 150 platforms in the Dutch part of the North Sea. Every day, several dozen helicopters fly there from Den Helder, bringing personnel and supplies. The number of people working on the manned production platforms ranges

from a couple of people up to several hundred. Besides technicians and operators there is often a cook and a paramedic as well. Some of the larger platforms have fitness centres and other recreational amenities on board.

New Niche for the Offshore Industry

Since the oil spillage disaster in the Gulf of Mexico, which began on 20 April 2010 when an explosion took place during experimental drilling being carried out by BP on drilling platform

The Deepwater Nautilus, sister rig to the Deepwater Horizon, out of the water, showing the full design of the rig including the underwater sections.

Deepwater Horizon, the oil industry has been cast in a bad light, and not for the first time. That is hardly surprising, for the oil disaster is the largest ever. Two days after the explosion, in which 11 workers lost their lives, the platform sank into the sea. As a consequence, large amounts of oil escaped into the sea water. To begin with, an amount was mentioned of 160,000 litres of oil per day, later that became 800,000 litres and later again it was reported that the scale of the disaster was even larger: apparently 60,000 vats of oil (9.5 million litres) flowed into the sea every day. The oil slick threatened the coasts of Florida, Louisiana and Alabama and caused enormous damage to the natural environment. The expectation was that the resulting decline in employment in the fishing and tourist sectors would be felt for decades to come.

Two Canadians hold signs at a demonstration on Parliament Hill imploring British Petroleum to do more to fix their oil spill problem in the Gulf of Mexico. Ottawa, Ontario 6 June 2010.

The accident was a disaster on an unprecedented scale, not just for the environment and tourism but for the oil industry itself as well. The financial, publicity and ecological damage grew daily and also brought risks for other energy concerns carrying out oil and gas exploration in the deep sea off the American coasts, such as the Anglo-Dutch Shell and the American Exxon Mobil.

It was particularly painful for BP because the company had been in the news in 2005 after a serious explosion in a refinery in Texas, where 15 people died and 500 were injured. BP has invested a great deal of energy in improving their safety policy in recent years, but the disaster in the Gulf of Mexico has once again resulted in serious damage to their reputation. Even so, BP senior executive Tony Hayward emphasized that deep-water drilling would continue in the USA despite the growing environmental and political backlash against the company. 'Apollo 13 (the unsuccessful third mission to the moon in 1970) did not stop the space race,' he told *The Guardian* newspaper. 'Neither did the Air France plane last year coming from Brazil (which mysteriously crashed) stop the world airline industry flying people around the world. It's the same for the oil industry.'[39]

Nonetheless, oil companies would be wise to increase public support by focusing on more sustainable developments as well. The companies that build drilling platforms for oil companies such as BP, Exxon and Shell have immense expertise in the field of building on open water. If they use that knowledge to develop floating buildings, they could be market leader in no time.

Two of the companies that came to the aid of the American government in combatting the oil disaster in the Gulf of Mexico were Dutch: dredging company Van Oord and research institute Deltares. That was no coincidence. The Netherlands is worldwide one of the largest players in

IN FLOATING URBAN DESIGN, THE OFFSHORE INDUSTRY AND THE BUILDING SECTOR FUSE TOGETHER

the field of building construction on the open sea. Fugro is one of the largest bureaus in the world in the field of seabed research, SBM Offshore is the market leader in the development and construction of floating production oil extraction platforms in deep water, Mammoet is the market leader in the field of heavy transport and hoisting activities, Smit International and Royal Boskalis Westminster (owner of Smit since 2010) are world leaders in the field of dredging. The Dutch-Swiss Allseas Marine Contractors is the world's largest seabed pipeline installer. So if there is expertise anywhere in the field of floating construction, it is in the Netherlands.[40]

But a lot needs to happen before this type of company can get involved in building floating cities on a large scale. And yet it is not just a pipedream. In floating urban design, the offshore industry and the building sector fuse together. The offshore industry will make platforms for urban use and construction companies will fabricate floating buildings. Before building on water can be a success, the rigid division between legislation relating to land and water needs to be abandoned. After all, there are new technologies available to turn water into building ground, so the effectiveness of old regulations needs to be examined to see if any strange situations have appeared. Holding on to superseded legislation leads only to frustration, not to innovation.

'Mare Liberum', Freedom of the Seas

Currently, international law makes a distinction between territorial waters and international 'free' waters. Territorial waters belong to the territory of the adjacent coastal nation. This state can exercise its sovereignty here and establish its own laws. Beyond the territorial waters is the free sea.

The market square in Delft with its statue of Hugo de Groot. In the background the Nieuwe Kerk (New Church), where he is buried.

The principle of free sea was formulated by Hugo de Groot, a lawyer from Delft. His *Mare Liberum* was published in 1609 in Leiden. De Groot was commissioned to write it by the Dutch East India Company when he was a young solicitor, to defend the conquest of a Portuguese warship. In the early seventeenth century, the United Kingdom of Spain and Portugal claimed a monopoly on trade with the East Indies. In 1604, after Admiral Jacob van Heemskerk had seized the Portuguese vessel Santa Catarina, the Dutch East India Company asked Grotius to produce a work legally defending the action on the grounds that, by claiming a monopoly on the right of trade, Spain-Portugal had deprived the Dutch of their natural trading rights. The work, *De Jure Praedae* (On the Law of Prize and Booty), remained unpublished during his lifetime, except for one chapter – in which Grotius defends free access to the ocean for all nations – which appeared under the famous title *Mare Liberum*. The work buttressed the Dutch position in the negotiations regarding the Twelve Years' Truce concluded that year with Spain, and was widely circulated and often reprinted.[41]

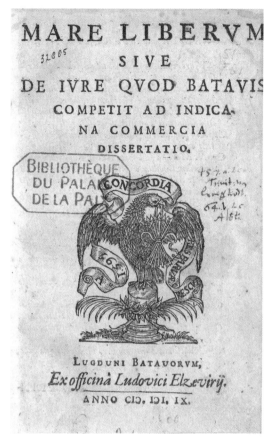

The Mare Liberum principle remained the ruling principle of international maritime trade for centuries. Even in 1918, after the First World War, the American president Woodrow Wilson reaffirmed the absolute freedom of shipping outside territorial waters in his Fourteen Points. However, many countries wanted to extend their territorial rights at sea, to the detriment of the free sea. Originally, the 'cannon shot rule' applied, which was formulated by Dutch lawyer Cornelis van Bijnkershoek. According to this rule, states could exercise their territorial rights up to three sea miles (5.5 km) from the coast, based on the maximum range of a cannonball fired from the coast. To meet the desire for expansion, the League of Nations held a conference in The Hague in 1930, but no agreement was reached there. Various countries began to unilaterally extend their sovereign rights at sea. Around 1967, only 25 countries were still using the original boundary of three sea miles; 66 nations had a 12-mile (22 km) boundary and eight had appropriated a 200-mile (370 km) boundary. In response, the United Nations organized a series of conferences, which resulted in the UN Convention on the Law of the Sea in 1994 by which the boundary of territorial waters was set at 12 miles.

Title page of *Mare Liberum*, written by Hugo de Groot. Translation of the Latin text: The Freedom of the Sea, a dissertation on the Right of the Dutch people to trade in East India, Leiden, Elsevier Publishers, 1609.

These days, Grotius' free sea is falling increasingly out of favour, not only because countries claim the right to exploit resources under the seabed (including oil and gas), but also because the freedom to fish out the world's seas is internationally justified by 'hiding behind Hugo de Groot's back', as the Utrecht Professor of Maritime Law Fred Soons put it in the *NRC Handelsblad* newspaper in December 2009.[42]

Treasure Hunt

The region that can be claimed by the coastal state for the extraction of resources is incidentally much larger than the territorial waters. Today, a country's marine economic area is defined by its Exclusive Economic Zone (EEZ), a 200-nautical-mile-wide strip of sea along the country's national coast line. This regulation, which was installed by the UN Convention on the Law of the Sea in 1982, grants a state special rights to exploit natural (such as oil) and marine (for instance fish) resources, including scientific research and energy production (wind farms, for example). In contrast with the situation in territorial waters, shipping traffic is free in the EEZ, just as sailing through international waters.

In practical terms, this means that if a country owns a minuscule rock somewhere in the ocean, this rock's exploitable surface increases from almost zero on-shore to 430,000 km^2 off-shore. If EEZs overlap, it is up to the states involved to delineate the actual boundaries; a rule that has led to decades of dispute in certain cases. Yet there will be even more underwater land to claim and there are more squabbles ahead: the 200-nautical-mile definition has been supplemented by a clause allowing expansion of the EEZ to the edge of the continental shelf. The first deadline for so-called 'continental shelf submissions' was passed in May 2009 and land (seabed) allocation is now underway. If underwater land grabbing goes on like this, the 'Freedom of the Seas' might soon be a thing of the past.[43]

At regular intervals, countries attempt to stretch the boundaries of their sovereign territory in such a way that economically interesting seabeds are located within their EEZ. In 2007, for instance, de Volkskrant newspaper reported a historic moment: the Russian explorer and member of parliament Artur Chilingarov planted a Russian flag on the seabed more than 4 km under the North Pole. Together with his team in two manned minisubmarines, he braved extreme cold, thick layers of ice and gigantic water pressure to press home Russian claims to the seabed. 'We can see yellowy ground around us; there is no sea life visible,' he told Russian news agency Itar-Tass.

Russia had a very good reason for making this expedition. It is likely that there are enormous supplies of minerals, oil and gas under the ice. In the past, no-one was concerned about the region because it was considered too expensive to drill under the surface of the North Pole. But exploitation of the area is becoming an increasingly interesting possibility due to the ice melting as a result of climate change, the high price of oil and the growing demand for fossil fuels from China and India in particular.

Russia is not the only country that would like to profit from the situation. Canada, the USA, Norway and Denmark (Greenland) also lay claim to this part of the ocean floor. Russia staked its claim in 2001: it considers the 2,000-km-long Lomonosov Reef that passes under the North Pole to be Russian territory. And if that immense reef is 'underwater Russia', the seabed can be exploited by Russia up to 200 miles from there. The Kremlin hoped that scientists taking part in the expedition would return with geological evidence that the reef does, in fact, belong to Russia.[44]

The United Nations would like to nip this sort of discussion in the bud and define the boundaries with the Commission on the Limits of the Continental Shelf. If the continental shelves are divided among the countries with a claim in a few decades time, and the freedom of the seas is actually limited to some extent, that would be a setback for free spirits such as Bates, Rosa and the members of the Seasteading Institute.

As a matter of fact, not just the rules for territorial waters lend themselves to creative interpretation, but also other components of maritime law. Seagoing ships are obliged to sail under a flag. The flag indicates the ship's nationality; flag transfer is only legally valid if transfer of ownership actually takes place. Originally, the reason for the flag was to indicate under which diplomatic protection the ship sailed on open waters, but since the seas have become increasingly easy and safe for

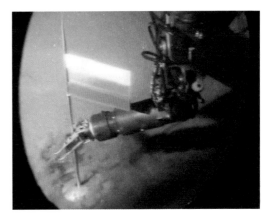

The manipulator arms of the Mir submersible plant the Russian flag on the ocean bed, 4 km under the North Pole.

The Mir submersible, which explorer Arthur Chilingarov used in 2007 to plant the Russian flag on the ocean bed. In this picture, the MIR is hoisted into the water via a cable connected to the ship's winch system. This front view shows the versatile manipulator arms and the huge viewing port.

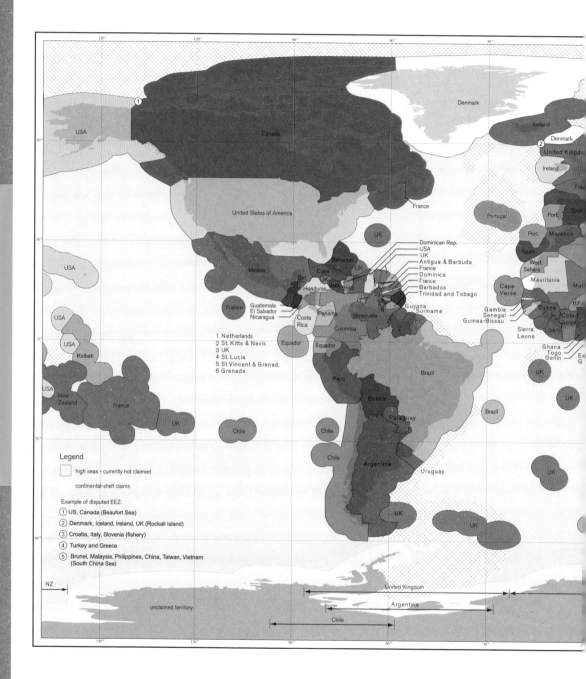

Map of the world showing all the Exclusive Economic Zones.

Legend

☐ high seas - currently not claimed

continental-shelf claims

Example of disputed EEZ:

① US, Canada (Beaufort Sea)

② Denmark, Iceland, Ireland, UK (Rockall Island)

③ Croatia, Italy, Slovenia (fishery)

④ Turkey and Greece

⑤ Brunei, Malaysia, Philippines, China, Taiwan, Vietnam (South China Sea)

1 Netherlands
2 St. Kitts & Nevis
3 UK
4 St. Lucia
5 St Vincent & Grenad.
6 Grenada

unclaimed territory

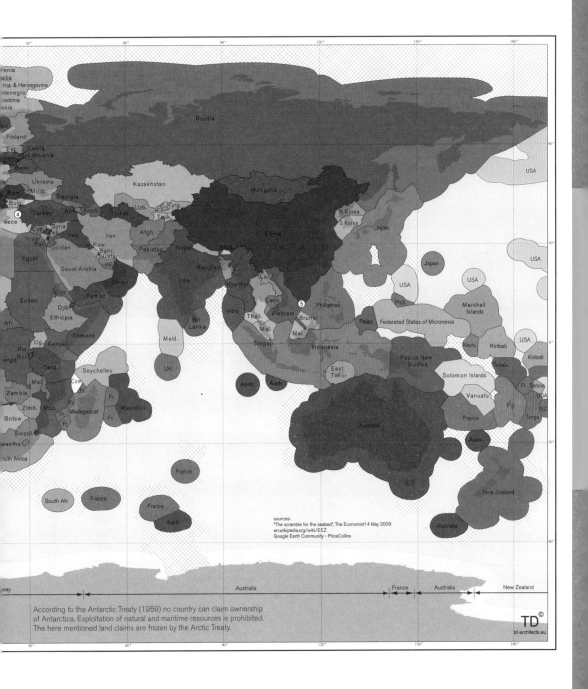

sources:
"The scramble for the seabed", The Economist 14 May 2009
en.wikipedia.org/wiki/EEZ
Google Earth Community - PriceCollins

According to the Antarctic Treaty (1959) no country can claim ownership
of Antarctica. Exploitation of natural and maritime resources is prohibited.
The here mentioned land claims are frozen by the Arctic Treaty.

TD©
td-architects.eu

shipping due to the progress made in communication and navigation technologies, fewer ship owners worry about protection. They would rather be led by economic motives when they register the ship. Some countries allow the registration of ships owned by foreigners under exceptionally attractive conditions. For instance, they offer significant tax advantages, they have few requirements in the area of social facilities for the crew or they only carry out limited checks that the safety rules are being adhered to. So, for instance, it is possible for Dutch ships to sail under the Antillean flag and German ships to sail under the flag of Antigua and Barbados. These so-called cheap flags (also called open registers) make it possible for many ships to sail under circumstances that leave a lot to be desired.

MANY REGULATIONS ON WATER ARE IN NEED OF THOROUGH REVIEW AND AMENDMENT

International law also contains a lot of gaps in the area of cabotage, with potential points of conflict as a result. Cabotage is the transport of goods or passengers between two points in the same country by a company from another country. In other words: cabotage is the right of a company from one country to trade in another country. Most countries do not allow cabotage by foreign companies. Originally, the cabotage rules were drawn up to promote national safety, but these days they are mainly fuelled by protectionist considerations. The rules relating to cabotage are therefore open to discussion these days in many cases. For this reason, the rules are being removed bit by bit within the European Union.

The current state of play with respect to open registers and cabotage provides an indication that the laws applicable on water were drawn up with intentions that do not correspond to the way in which the rules are being interpreted these days. Many regulations on water are therefore in need of thorough review and amendment.

A New Legal Status for Buildings

As shown by the previously quoted example of the houseboat resident in Almere and the SS Rotterdam, the difference between moveable and fixed types of housing is completely outdated. House are houses, even if they can be moved. It is already possible to regard ships and water houses as fixed objects now. Land houses on the other hand are not necessarily fixed and can also be designated as moveable. Defining water houses in advance as ships does not help large-scale development of floating urban components. The legal question should not be: Does the object float or is it located on solid ground? The only relevant question is: Is the object intended for permanent residence or not? The most predictable opposition, for instance from mortgage lenders who want easily traceable collateral for their loan, is that floating objects are moveable and therefore less creditworthy. There is an argument that can be used here: just as buildings are recorded in the land register, ships are signed into the ship's register. In the ideal situation, both registers could be merged.

A New Legal Status for Districts on and under Water

Just as new developments in the field of floating construction can tempt individuals to a certain interpretation of the law that means they do not have to pay taxes, gaps in the maritime regulations can likewise stimulate countries to enlarge their territory in a creative way. As described above, Russia is trying to expand its territory by laying claim to a 2,000-km-long reef and in so doing gaining the right to exploit the treasures under the seabed. Until something has been established about the division of rights on the continental shelf, every country can lay similar claims. If the powerplay employed by important countries such as Canada, Russia and the USA goes on long enough, this urge for expansion will escalate whenever one of the parties feels unfairly treated due to misuse of new technologies by one of the other big players. Just as the conflict between the Netherlands and Spain-Portugal at the beginning of the seventeenth century led to the first international legislation for the open sea, new legislation that goes much further will emerge as a consequence of the international struggle for fossil fuels in the seabed.

Interesting hypothetical situations could also arise during this process. What would happen, for instance, if floating constructions really could belong to the territory of a country? If the floating islands in the Maldives are implemented as planned, will that mean that the islands – a substantial and densely-populated part of the country – could, over time, be moored off the coast of, say, Sri Lanka, when the sea level has risen and the original islands have vanished? Could Russia use islands to press home its claim to the Lomonosov Reef, simply by mooring them above the reef? In that case, could floating islands also be used in political scuffles, for instance between population groups that deny each other the right to live in a particular country?

And what would happen if floating islands were not national territory? For example, would that mean that a floating park moored in the Hudson next to Manhattan would not belong to the USA? Or would it belong to national territory inside the territorial waters, but not beyond these waters? And what about Greenland, for instance? Ice covers 80 per cent of the surface area of this island, some of which is buoyant, and large ice floes break off regularly. Is a broken-off ice floe still part of Greenland? And who is responsible if the floe causes any damage?

These are interesting questions, to which no clear answers are possible at present. One thing that is clear is that the buoyancy technologies available at the moment justify new hybrid legislation. These new regulations will encourage the expansion of urban space onto the water and simultaneously regulate territorial expansion of states onto water, with the corresponding exploitation of the seabed. Furthermore, the new freedoms offered by the dynamism of the water will increase the flexibility and adaptability of urban components in the future.

IT'S UP

TO THE

CLIMAT

E-CHAN

GE GEN

ERATIO

Chapter 9

MOMENTUM

Bill Gates, figurehead and founder of computer software producer Microsoft, told an anecdote during the British launch of Windows Vista in 2007 about a special purchase he had made 13 years earlier. 'I remember going home one night and telling my wife Melinda that I was going to buy a notebook,' he told Lynne Brindley, the director of the British Library in London, where the launch took place. 'She didn't think that was a very big deal. I said, no, this is a pretty special notebook. This is the *Codex Leicester*, one of Leonardo da Vinci's notebooks. I have always been amazed by him. He would work by drawing things and writing down his ideas about how light worked, how water worked, how weapons would work. He designed all sorts of flying machines, like helicopters, way before you could actually build something like that.'[45]

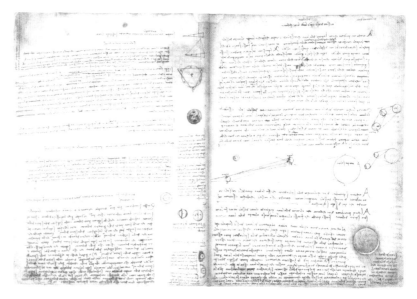

Leonardo da Vinci wrote the *Codex Leicester* in the period 1508-1510. The manuscript consists of 18 double-folded sheets with notes and sketches, written mirror-wise. In the codex, Da Vinci noted his observations and theories in relation to rivers and sea, the properties of water, stone and fossils, air and natural light. He dealt with four themes: architecture, painting, human anatomy and mechanics. Bill Gates bought the book in 1994 for 30.8 million dollars.

Gates has made no secret of his fascination for Leonardo da Vinci on other occasions, either. Microsoft's senior executive has looked up to the Renaissance man in admiration since he was 10 years old. So in 1994, he had plenty of money to spare to buy the notebook: 30.8 million US Dollars.

Da Vinci was the prototype of the universal human being. He was accomplished in every area of science, art, anatomy, architecture and philosophy, and had furthermore a clear vision in all these areas. Even more than an inventor, Leonardo was a visionary. Not only his far-reaching ideas are proof of that, but also the way he worked. According to most of the biographies he always made an enthusiastic start on a new topic, but he rarely finished his work. For him, the most important thing was not the physical result of his ideas, but the broadening of his insight.

The weapons, helicopters and submarines he dreamt up are standard components of society today, but in the sixteenth century they were revolutionary. They could have changed the world as it was then, but that didn't happen. That was because they were far above the powers of imagination of his contemporaries, there was no demand for his products and the state of technology was not advanced enough to realize the designs easily. After all, what was the point of a submarine or a tank in a world where the horse-drawn cart was the most important means of transport? Leonardo da Vinci's ideas lacked momentum, unlike Bill Gates' ideas. The world was not ready for them yet.

Regardless of how good an idea is, it needs the right environment to be understood and taken into use. In order to be a success, the idea has to meet a number of criteria. First of all, it has to be realizable with technologies that are already available. The intended users have to be able to absorb the leap of innovation. The ideas need a communication channel and they must have political support. Good communication channels are more important than they might appear at first sight. It is entirely possible that totally brilliant solutions to significant problems are gathering dust in attics. They will never reach the general public – or at any rate, not in time.

The requirement for new products and services generally follows on from big changes in society and the living environment. For instance, climate change has created demand for a whole range of innovations; solar cells, hybrid cars, biofuel and renewed interest in nuclear energy are just a few examples. Sudden social upheavals and wars often bring about innovations. Jet engines for aircraft, for example, were developed for fighter planes during the Second World War and are now used on a large scale in civil aviation. The same is true of a considerable number of global positioning system (GPS) technologies used routinely by almost every car driver in his vehicle, and for the satellites everyone with a mobile phone uses on a daily basis.

If there is no demand for an invention, it can be created. A strong vision can completely change the perception the masses have of an existing product. Apple boss Steve Jobs introduced the first iPhone in 2007. The mobile phone with touchscreen was revolutionary. During his presentation, Jobs imagined the new world that would open up to iPhone users. To the surprise of many people, you could buy apps (applications) and download them via web shops.

(Top)
Martin Cooper, the inventor of the cell phone, made the first analogue mobile phone call in the USA on a larger prototype model in 1973. This is a re-enactment in 2007.

(Bottom)
The iPhone 3G was introduced on 11 July 2008, 35 years after Cooper made the first mobile telephone call. Telephoning is just a side issue with the iPhone; you can use it to read the newspaper, send e-mails, take photos, watch videos or download one of the tens of thousands of applications.

Before the smartphone without a keyboard was available, no-one missed a piece of equipment that was somewhere in between a computer, an iPod and a mobile phone, but the iPhone quickly became the benchmark for all other telephone manufacturers. Apple had combined existing markets and products to create something completely new and made such a good job of it that market demand for mobile phones has definitively changed since then. Inventors provide a solution to an existing problem. Successful visionaries are capable of creating a new requirement. Visionary entrepreneurs like Steve Jobs can create a requirement and fill that gap with their products.

Creativity is essential to develop new products: you need to make a connection between things that are generally seen as belonging to separate worlds. Visionaries hardly

REGARDLESS OF HOW GOOD AN IDEA IS, IT NEEDS THE RIGHT ENVIRONMENT TO BE TAKEN INTO USE

ever invent something original, but make new combinations of existing products or services. Facebook and Twitter came into being because a few smart people merged two or more already available technologies into a new product. The developers of the new services are brilliant at combining ideas and subsequently turning them into a product that even manages to create a new market. These people are not conventional thinkers; they are able to let go of existing perceptions and achieve cross-overs that create a new requirement.

Bill Gates' software was not new either. However, he saw the possibilities for practical application, more so than others. If Gates had been born 10 years earlier, he would probably have been no more than a highly gifted visionary, and not the rich entrepreneur he is today. In his case, everything fell into place at just the right moment. The rise of programming, the logistically increasingly complex society and the growing availability of the computer created the right momentum for him. When Gates bought the *Codex Leicester*, he understood perhaps better than anyone else that he was blessed with the right date of birth, unlike Leonardo da Vinci. For was it not Da Vinci who made the first sketches for a mechanical calculator, and did the calculator not ultimately form the basis for every personal computer?

Ideas for Living on Water Lacked Momentum

If you take this train of thought a little further, you might come to the conclusion that new ideas do not exist at all. The only thing that keeps changing, and is therefore new, is the context within which human beings operate. The continually changing context ensures that the same idea does lead to successful application in one decade, but comes to nothing in a different decade.

Ideas for living on water did not surface in the last 10 years. People have lived on and next to water for centuries. The Thai architect Sumet Jumsai even claims that it is perfectly possible that the first habitat ever built by human hands was a floating house. 'It is probably not a coincidence that cultural historians of South-East Asia agree on the fact that humans first settled along sea shores and only later moved inland,' he wrote in *Architecture and Identity*. 'Some original oceanic migrations are evident, so that Thor Heyerdahl in turn can say with confidence (in his book *Early Man and the Ocean*) that the first man-made vehicle was the boat, or the raft. At the risk of jumping to conclusions, I will state that the first man-made habitat was the house on a raft.'[46]

Human beings are inclined to forget the past quickly, so ideas often come across as new and original. But nothing could be further from the truth. In the twentieth century, too, various architects made large-scale plans for living on water. But the context was not present for realization of the plans every time the ideas appeared on the drawing board.

As long ago as the 1960s and 1970s, for instance, Archigram, Richard Buckminster Fuller, Jacques Rougerie and

UTOPIA

Map of the world showing
the lost continents Mu,
Atlantis and Lemuria, as
well as a list of utopian
designs. Proposals for
cities on water (in blue)
are from all times, with a
clear concentration in the
20th century, but missed
momentum up until now.

Freudenstadt, by Heinrich Schickhardt (1599-1604)
Emulating Vitruvius, by Daniele Barham (1560)   New Atlantis, by Sir Francis Bacon (1624)
The Ideal Town and the Round Fortress, by Albrecht Durer(1528)   The Standardized City, Simon Stevin (1594)   Domus Aurea Neronis, by Johann Fischer von
Tenochtitlan, by Cortes (1524) The Fortress Cities, by P. Cataneo (1554)Pamphagonia, by Bishop J. Hall (1605)   The City Tower and Babylon, by A.Kircher (1679)   Plans for Chaux, by Le
The Water City, by Leonardo Da Vinci (1500) I Mondi, by Anton F. Doni (1552)The colective Ideal City, by G. Vassari the Younger (1598)   Emperor's Adrian Rome, by Franciscus Contini (1668)   Shipwreck of the fle
Several Theathre Cities (1500 - 1600).   Macaria (island), Caspar Stiblin (1555) City of Truth (Civitas Veri), by Bartolomeo del Bene (1609)   The Habsburg Dream / Schonbrunn (1656 - 1723)   Ideal City in the Sea, by Bernardo
Sforzinda, by Filarete (1465) A City on Several Levels, by Leonardo Da Vinci (1485)   The Wise and Insane World, by F. Doni (1553) The City of the Sun, by Tommaso Campanella (1602)   The Tower City, by Athanasius Kircher (1664)   St. Petersburg, by Le Blond and Homann (1717)
Model Cities, by Giorgio Martini and others (1475 -1590)   The City of Hochelaga, by Jacques Cartier (1556)   The Citadel Towns, by J. Perret (1601) Felsenburg Island, by Johann Schnabel (1646)   Fortress Towns, by European builders (1700/20) Fantastical Rome, by G. B
The Hypnerotomachia Pliphili, by Francesco Colonna (1499)   A Fortified Town, by D. Speckle (1589)   The Oval City, by Joseph F. Elder (1650)   Karlsruhe, by Durlach and Weinbrenner (1715 - 1800)
The City of Perspective, by Piero della Francesca (1480)   Military Architecture, by F. Marchi (1570)   Wilhelmostadum, by Adrian Antonisz (1647)   The Garden City Azilia in Georgia, by Robert Montgomery
Utopia Island, by Thomas More (1516)   The Geometric City, by Vicenzo Scamozzi (1615)   A Baroque Jerusalem, by Jihann Herz (1730)
Geometric Fortification, by Castriotto and Maggi (1564) Ideal Fortress Town, by Robert Fluss (1617)
The True Society, by B. del Bene (1565 - 1609)   Christianopolis, by Johannes V. Andreae (1619)

Mu

The concept and the name Mu were proposed
by 19th century traveler and writer Augustus Le
Plongeon, who claimed that several ancient
civilizations, such as those of Egypt and
Mesoamerica, were created by refugees from
Mu — which he located in the Atlantic Ocean.

Atlantis

Atlantis is a legendary island first mentioned in Plato's
dialogues Timaeus and Critias. In his account, Atlantis
was a naval power lying "in front of the Pillars of
Hercules" that conquered many parts of Western
Europe and Africa approximately 9600 BC. After a
failed attempt to invade Athens, Atlantis sank into the
ocean "in a single day and night of misfortune".

1500   1600   1700

Lemuria

The concept of Lemuria has been adopted by writers involved in the occult, as well as some Tamil writers of India. Accounts of Lemuria differ, but all share a common belief that a continent existed in ancient times and sank beneath the ocean as a result of a geological, often cataclysmic, change.

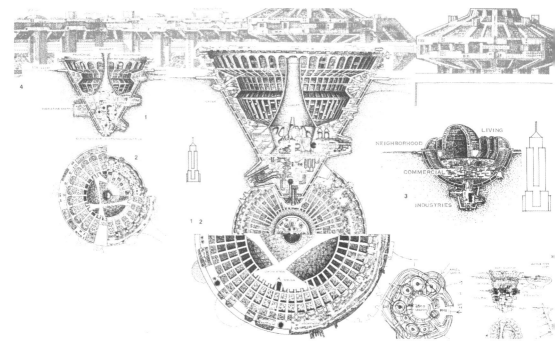

Paolo Soleri, Novanoah 2,
a floating city for 2.4
million people, 1964.

Jacques Rougerie,
Thallasopolis 2, a floating,
seagoing and nomadic
university situated in
the North Atlantic,
published in 'Habiter
La Mer', l'Architecture
d'Aujourd'hui 175
(September/October 1974).

Metabolists such as Kenzo Tange and Kiyonori Kikutake put forward the notion of floating cities. Their proposals did not drop out of thin air. It was not just interest in the primitive floating living communities in Asia and South America that occasioned these designs. 'Funding for oceanography from national military agencies since the early to the mid-1950s ensured that oceanography was a 'dynamic growth industry' by the early 1960s,' Peter Raisbeck wrote in *Marine and Underwater Cities 1960-1975*.

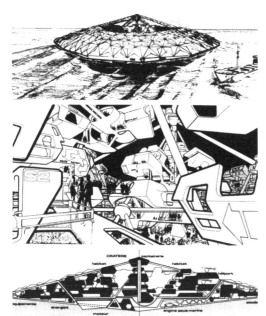

Many architects became fascinated by this new research field – which was mainly being explored for military and economic reasons – and made designs for living communities on and under water. Warren Chalk, one of the six members of Archigram, published his 'Underwater City project of 1964' in *Archigram* no. 5: 'A megastructure of diagonal tubes connected by spheres and completely under water.' On that same spread was the Marine City designed by Kikutake and Buckminster Fuller's Underwater Island of 1963.

ALVIN- undersea research craft
TURTLE-Deep submermergence submarine capable of exploring ocean bed
COUSTEAU-Underwater vill prototype for an underwa city.
DEEPSTAR
INAUT biggest undersea arch submarine
NAVY underwater laboratory
COUSTEAU-Underwater house
UNDERWATER
HARDWARE

Spread from *Archigram* 5 (1964), showing examples of Cold War underwater vehicles including Sealab, Alvin, Turtle, Aluminaut, Deepstar and Cousteau's vertically aligned underwater house.

Although the proposals here were mainly for living communities under water, there were more visions at that time for floating cities. One well-known example is Kenzo Tange's 1960 Tokyo Bay project, in which he proposed extending the Japanese capital into the bay, by means of a structuralistically designed mega-expansion that was partly buoyant. In the same year, he designed the floating 'Community Plan for 25,000 people' for the harbour in Boston. Buckminster Fuller came up with Triton City in 1967, a floating city for 100,000 inhabitants, similarly intended for Tokyo Bay. Buckminster Fuller distinguished three types of floating cities. Each type was to be located in relation to a particular geography: one type for protected harbour cities such as Triton City, another for semi-protected waters or deep-sea types and yet another deep-sea type – spherical and cylindrical geodesic floating cities whose 'hulls' were below the sea. [48]

These floating cities never made it off the drawing board. They were well ahead of their time but they eventually lacked the positive attitude of architecture critics, as well as technological possibilities for realization. There was already

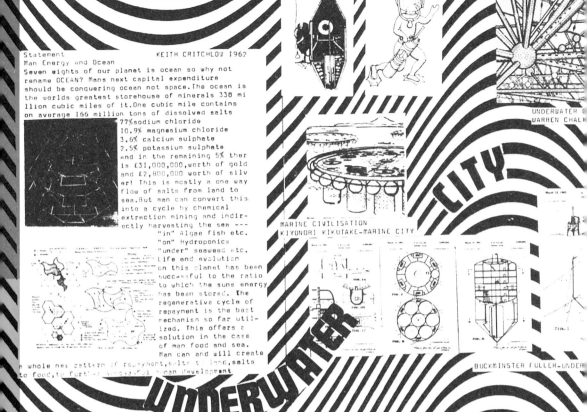

Statement   KEITH CRITCHLOW 1962
Man Energy and Ocean
Seven eights of our planet is ocean so why not
rename OCEAN? Mans next capital expenditure
should be conquering ocean not space.The ocean is
the worlds greatest storehouse of minerals 330 mi
llion cubic miles of it.One cubic mile contains
on average 166 million tons of dissolved salts
              77%sodium chloride
              10.9% magnesium chloride
              3.6% calcium sulphate
              2.5% potassium sulphate
              And in the remaining 5% ther
              is £31,000,000,worth of gold
              and £2,600,000 worth of silv
              er! This is mostly a one way
              flow of salts from land to
              sea.But man can convert this
              into a cycle by chemical
              extraction mining and indir-
              ectly harvesting the sea ---
                    "in" Algae fish etc.
                    "on" Hydroponics
                    "under" seaweed etc.
              Life and evolution
              on this planet has been
              successful to the ratio
              to which the suns energy
              has been stored. The
              regenerative cycle of
              repayment is the best
              mechanism so far util-
              ized. This offers a
              solution in the case
              of man food and sea.
              Man can and will create
h whole new pattern of repayment,salts t land,salts
to food,to further successful human development

MARINE CIVILISATION
KIYONORI KIKUTAKE-MARINE CITY

UNDERWATER
WARREN CHALK

CITY

UNDERWATER

BUCKMINSTER FULLER-UNDER

Spread from *Archigram 5*
(1964), showing a number
of marine and underwater
projects: Kikutake's
Marine City, Buckminster
Fuller's 1963 Underwater
Island, Warren Chalk's
'Underwater City project
of 1964' and a statement by
Keith Critchlow.

criticism of the utopian designs of this generation of architects in the first half of the 1970s. According to accounts,
Buckminster Fuller was jeered off the platform by students
during a visit to London in 1972 as an apolitical amoral
technocrat, and that criticism was directed at more of his
contemporaries. If you look at the designs for the floating
cities, you can probably understand the reactions: they are
both impressive and megalomaniac, and do not show enough
consideration for the living requirements of the individual.
Furthermore, there was no structured step-by-step plan
indicating how it would be possible to progress from the
city in its current state to the visionary cities envisaged by
the architects.

One way to get large plans accepted is to indicate
how the desired result can be achieved in various phases.
That takes the proposals out of the realm of unachievable
utopias into visions of the future with a sense of reality. It
is important to come out with incremental solutions: each
stage goes one step further than the previous one, so the
final situation does not come as a surprise. As said before,

individuals are often flexible, but changing the perception of the masses is a slow process. A thin thread breaks if you pull on it too hard and too fast. But the most ponderous seagoing ship eventually starts to move if you exercise force on it slowly with a thick cable. If Buckminster Fuller and Kenzo Tange had described the gradual construction of their floating cities in a time perspective of, say, 50 years, then Tokyo might have looked very different by now.

However, the studies were not totally without results; their influence on the developed environment was certainly tangible. Kiyonori Kikutake, for example, realized the Aquapolis platform off the coast of Okinawa,

Kenzo Tange, A plan for Tokyo Bay, 1960.

which functioned as the centrepiece of Expo 75. This expo was organized on the occasion of the transfer of Okinawa from the USA to Japan, and focused on oceanographic technologies, marine life and oceanic cultures. The motto was 'The sea we would like to see'. The Aquapolis was constructed at a shipyard in Hiroshima, Japan, and then towed to the Expo site. It was 32 m high, and had a 100-m² deck. After the Expo was over, the Aquapolis was retained as an attraction and

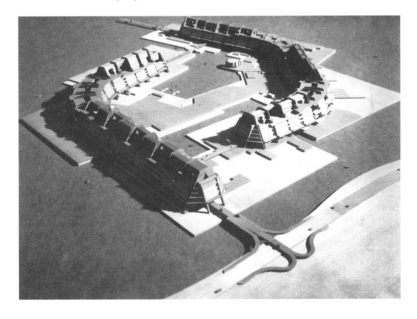

Kenzo Tange, Community plan for 25,000 people (also known as the MIT Boston Harbour Project), 1960.

Richard Buckminster Fuller,
Triton City, a tetrahedral
floating city for Tokyo Bay,
1967.

Kiyonori Kikutake,
Aquapolis platform at
Expo 75 off the coast
of Okinawa, Japan.

eventually hosted four million visitors. As the years passed,
the number of visitors to the Aquapolis declined and it was
closed in 1993. In October 2000, the Aquapolis was towed
away to Shanghai to be scrapped.

Nevertheless, the designs from the 1960s and 1970s
did have an influence on the way our urban living environments look today, in a more sustainable sense. There is a
direct line between Tange's 1960 design for Tokyo Bay, by
way of the Pampus plan designed by Van den Broek & Bakema
in 1964 for the Amsterdam expansion district IJburg – built

Van den Broek en Bakema,
Plan Pampus, design for
a series of artificially
constructed islands in
the IJmeer to the east
of Amsterdam, 1964.

completely on artificially constructed
islands – to the design that served as
the basis on which the islands were
ultimately constructed. In this district,
the first floating neighbourhoods in the
Netherlands realized in one fell swoop
by a municipality have been achieved.
They are described as an urban design
innovation, but are in fact a watered-
down version of what was once designed as a dynamic floating city in a
different context.

The fact that there was no
momentum in the past for floating

cities, does not mean that that is still true today. In many ways, the current period can no longer be compared with the situation in the 1960s and 1970s. The context in which ideas for floating cities appear has changed radically in the last 50 years. Technologies are more advanced, judging by the patent Dutch Docklands has been granted worldwide for 'the production method for large floating constructions'.

Society also has to deal with altered circumstances. Climate change and a rising sea level were still unknown concepts in the 1960s, but have by now forced society to assess 'new' technologies for climate adaptation with an open mind. Unexpected natural phenomena, whether or not related to climate change, have a more profound impact on society than they would have had a few decades ago. That is because Western society these days is organized in such a way that a small disturbance in the balance can have far-reaching consequences. Modern people are completely dependent on technology, but are usually only aware of it when the technology fails. When that happens, insecurity spreads. As a result, politicians and citizens must be receptive to a more flexible society.

The Vulnerable Society

On 14 April 2010 the Eyjafjallajökull volcano erupted in Iceland. It was not the first eruption that year – that was on 20 March – but up until then the most violent. If you look

for photos on the Internet, you can get an impression of the calamitous force involved in the eruption. Red fountains of incandescent magma shot upwards out of the crater. Glacier ice – turned instantaneously into steam by the heat – created white plumes of smoke above the volcano. Released melt-water raised the water level in the Markarfljót River by 3 m within a couple of hours. A state of emergency was declared immediately in Iceland. Because of the flood danger, 500 farmers and their families were evacuated from the regions south of the volcano.[49]

In the following days, the rest of Europe was also faced with the consequences. The volcano ash from the eruption that landed in the atmosphere caused serious disruptions to aviation. West European air space was closed because the volcano ash could damage aircraft engines. From that moment onwards, 63,000 flights were cancelled and tens of thousands of passengers were stranded. The total damage to aviation was estimated at 1.26 billion euros in lost turnover. That is excluding the costs incurred by the airlines to provide their passengers with things like accommodation, food and drink, and road transport. The claims amounting to millions made by the duped travellers later were not included in that amount, either.[50]

The consequences of the natural phenomena were interesting. Just like the Tsunami in 2004, the ash cloud in 2010 brought about a change in the way people looked at the world around them. The media played an important role here, but a large number of people were also directly confronted with the consequences. The Japanese architect Akihisa Hirata, for example, landed unintentionally and reluctantly in Italy, where he was stuck for a while. Afterwards, he told his story in architecture magazine *Mark*: 'I ended up in Rome, where I visited the city's ancient remains, which give the place such a rich character. The situation there is completely different from that in Tokyo, where things change and renew so quickly. The volcanic eruption made me realize that nature can disrupt the systems of today's world so easily. It made me want to think more about the greatness of nature and history.'[51]

In this way, natural phenomena contribute to a feeling that modern society is perhaps not organized in the best possible way, and that there are better solutions for the problems of this time. That feeling of urgency creates a momentum to implement new visions. For example, it is possible that the ash cloud will create the momentum to develop electric aircraft, or that propeller aeroplanes will make a comeback.

The Internet as Democratic Spreader of New Ideas

In order to create momentum for a new idea, a good communication channel is very important, as described above. For decades, architects and urban designers had to rely on publications in magazines, which were part of commercial businesses and therefore had to focus on the greatest common denominator to achieve high sales figures. As a result, they concentrated mainly on the establishment. Admission to the establishment took years of effort and involved lobbying the media for attention. Furthermore, magazines were mainly looking for realized work, because that provided the most attractive images which in turn increased saleability. Many a young architect had to rack his brains to figure out a way to get his work and ideas published.

In the last decade, three impulses have changed the traditional communication channels for architects. Modern visualization technologies, online media (including architecture blogs in particular) and social networks are the most important means these days to spread new ideas and bring them to people's attention. The illustration and spreading of architectural production have been democratized as a result.

To illustrate ideas, easy-to-use 3D visualization programmes are now available in the shape of software such as Maya, 3ds Max, Rhino and Sketchup, so that designs can come to life with minimal effort. The pictures seem so real that photos of realized buildings are no longer necessary to change the public's perception. In addition, increasingly realistic video games and animation films lead to young people absorbing new ideas much more quickly than older people. Much more so than previous generations, they are growing up with the idea that unimaginable living environments are the most normal thing in the world.

Blogs also play a significant role in increasing awareness of the possibilities for building on water. The rise of the Internet and the blog revolution have had a liberating effect, while traditional publishers are still having a difficult time, in financial terms. Anyone who wants to tell, imagine or change can present his or her ideas on the Internet, without the intervention of a publisher earning money from distribution or advertising. The Internet is a podium open to everyone.

New ideas spread incredibly fast these days, through the almost endless growth of social networks. Notions are immediately praised or criticized based on their virtual appearance. They grow further, become stronger and find supporters, or they fade away and die. In this way, the Internet provides an evolutionary acceleration of the exchange of ideas and has made architecture – and many other fields – more accessible as a result. Architecture has become public property: a consumer item to provide instant satisfaction. That is not a threat but a huge opportunity for everyone convinced of the truth of their plans.

Once you understand the rules of the game, you can turn the process around as well. You can use social networks to generate support for your ideas and, in so doing, contribute to a change of perception. They provide the opportunity to close the gap between vision and reality. Online media are the driving force behind change as a result.

From about 2005, a growing number of designs for floating buildings appeared on the blogs and websites of architecture firms, as an answer to the climate problem. The simultaneous appearance of the same idea seems like a form of serendipity, in which individuals in different places in the world think they have found a solution, independent of others, to rising sea levels. But serendipity has nothing to do with it. To use the words of British author Peter Russell, the Internet works like a 'global brain': a form of collective intelligence that is organized in a similar way to the human brain. Leonardo da Vinci had to work out and imagine his ideas alone – he was a voice in the wilderness. But now, thousands of like-minded people are busy working on a gigantic collaborative project: investigating the possibilities offered by building on water and overcoming the problems that arise. Everyone influences everyone else. That leads to a steady growth in the information available and in turn to more credibility for the proposed solutions.

SWOT

So these 'global brainers' work out the possibilities of living on water, on the basis of a few strong visions of the future. Bit by bit they are closing the gap between daily practice and the image of the future. Besides a wealth of possibilities, there is also a series of problem areas that could constitute a threat to the coming-of-age of the market for floating construction, if they are not resolved. A SWOT analysis based on the previous chapters produces the following strengths, weaknesses, opportunities and threats for building on water.

Strengths

The strengths of building on water have been covered in depth by now and can be summarized in a few points. Building on water is a means of carrying out responsible water management, by which the consequences of rising sea levels can be tackled by taking the offensive. One obvious strength is the double use of space. In almost all urban regions, more space is needed for water collection, and with floating buildings, living, green spaces and other urban functions can be combined with water storage. The possibility for separating the construction site and the final location, by transporting the building over water after it is completed, has the advantage of more efficient, cheaper and cleaner building. After all, the new-build comes sailing in and is operational at once. The surroundings are spared the disturbance of months of building

One of the advantages
of floating buildings: the
construction location
is not the same as the
final mooring location.
As a result, the building
process can take place in a
controlled environment and
the future neighbours are
spared the nuisance caused
by building activities.

and the final appearance is immediately achieved. The last of
the most self-evident strengths is the fact that floating buildings do not leave any scars on their building locations, and
that minimizes the carbon footprint during their lifespans and
the physical footprint afterwards.

Weaknesses

At the moment, the main weakness of floating buildings is
the fact that relatively few projects have been realized that
go beyond the scale of a houseboat. There are not enough
reference projects with a high urban density. That has negative consequences for the general price-making process.
Existing projects provide very little to go on for both building contractors and customers when estimating the costs of
construction. Costs and profit cannot be calculated in advance
with complete clarity, and that curbs the growth of the
market. This disadvantage will disappear of its own accord
in time, as building production on water increases.

Another weakness is that the general public's change
in perception is happening slowly. Because urban living on
water once began with inferior cheap building materials,
which did not compare favourably with the quality of building
materials on land, the general public finds it difficult to accept
what is actually an incorrect image, and that perception is
slow to change.

Opportunities

The opportunities appear to be endless and are not yet visible in their full breadth. In the coming years, the combination of different disciplines and building technologies will lead to cross-overs, in which new products and functions on water will come into being. The opportunities that have already crystallized are new density and new flexibility for urban environments. Higher density is necessary to retain the level of prosperity of every growing city. New flexibility makes reconfiguration of urban structures possible on water. Floating urban components also provide sustainable solutions for food, energy and water and make more efficient use of the supply of buildings possible, because their technical lifespan can be completely served out. After all, they can be traded and relocated, just like any other product. One last significant opportunity is the revival of private transport over water. Water provides possibilities for buoyant means of transport and for floating roads, both of which can take the pressure off the existing infrastructure on land.

Threats

And then there are the threats. A niche market slowly developing into a growth market cannot avoid coming across a series of threats. The greatest threats are principally all the factors that make living on water different from living on land. In simple terms: if living on water has the same costs, quality and comfort as on land, there are no threats left to speak of. We will examine the three points in turn.

First of all, the costs. Op paper, they are similar to building on land. Construction techniques can vary, but as the water market grows, that will not be translated into the price. In urban components, only the foundations are essentially different from their equivalents on land. In terms of costs, buoyant foundations are similar to filled-in land or foundation piles. Building on water is financially feasible at locations where building land is expensive and where there is little or no alternative space on land. But as long as building on water remains a niche, the illusion of an inflated price will hang above the market as a threat.

Secondly, the quality of floating buildings. Lack of quality as a threat does not have much to do with lifespan and construction quality. Both are guaranteed anyway because the official building requirements for floating buildings are the same as on land. Lack of quality has mainly to do with the current appearance of buildings on the water. It is the threat of what you could call 'freak' architecture. The designers who created floating living communities in the 1960s and 1970s now have their own imitators who still work on the strangest utopian projects in the margins of architecture production. Their ideas are certainly likeable, but they do not contribute to a general acceptance of the idea that building on water can be a structural and sustainable solution to our society's problems.

Users need to accept the appearance of technological innovations before the innovation can become a success. That will only work in the first place if the innovations fall within the reference framework of the intended users. When Carl Benz equipped his Patent-Motorwagen with a petrol engine in 1886, it still looked like a carriage, so as not to scare the brave riders when they raced over the German roads at a top speed of 16 km/h. It took decades of gradual adaptations before cars took on the aerodynamic shapes we know today.

This pattern is also visible in the history of architecture. During the course of the twentieth century, buildings have been filled with an increasing number of technical installations: to begin with, houses were already considered to be advanced if they were equipped with electricity, running water and a sewer system, but later more and more advanced communication facilities and air-conditioning installations were added and in recent years, all sorts of domotica. But when architects decided it was about time to put all these installations on display and high-tech architecture was born, it did not attract very many clients. High-tech architecture never really filtered through to house construction, partly because most people do not want to be constantly reminded of the fact that they live in a technological installation. 'La maison est une machine à habiter,' said Le Corbusier, but that doesn't

The 1886 Benz Patent-Motorwagen, equipped with the first single-cylinder four-stroke piston engine. The car was not a converted carriage, but a completely independent design.

mean it has to look like one as well. The same is true for
floating buildings. To make floating living acceptable to the
masses, a floating district will first of all need to look just like
a traditional neighbourhood. The foundations of a building do
not have any influence on the image and functioning of the
occupants. It must be possible to park beside the house and
gardens need to be a normal component of the infrastructure.
A building with buoyant foundations needs to reassure and
seduce traditionally minded users, instead of scaring them off.

And thirdly, there is the question of the comfort level
of buildings on water. Many people who have never been
inside a floating water villa associate these houses with damp,
cold and disturbing movements caused by the rippling water.
However, a pleasant interior climate is no longer a problem.

A pleasant interior climate
for floating houses is no
longer a problem. All the
technical facilities can be
exactly the same as on
land. Floating house with
two storeys in Amsterdam
designed by David Keuning.

All the facilities in the area of cooling, heating and ventilation can be exactly the same as on land, and all the other technical factors that guarantee a comfortable indoor climate are in general use. The only item that could still threaten the congeniality of the accommodation is the question of stability.

Stability comfort is determined by the amount of listing and increase in movement of the floating object, and by fluctuation of the water level. As a result, stability depends mainly on the size of the structure and the local characteristics of the water. It goes without saying that the amount of movement of a large building in inner-city water cannot be detected.

However, on open water that can be very different. Floating buildings do not necessarily satisfy the comfort targets that are imposed on buildings on land. On open water, where there can be swells with a frequency of 15 seconds and waves can reach a height of 1 m, additional stabilization techniques are necessary to achieve the same level of comfort as on land. That might sound complicated, but that too is a question of perception. Stability comfort for many buildings on land is not a matter of course either.

Skyscrapers, for example, decorate the skyline of almost every American and Asian metropolis. They provide accommodation to sometimes thousands of residents or employees, people who walk in and out of the buildings every day as though it were the most normal thing in the world.

The upper storeys of the former Twin Towers in New York were evacuated during storms, because people working in one tower could feel their own tower moving and see the other tower swaying.

But if a storm rises, skyscrapers sway to and fro. The higher and narrower the building is, the more severely the movement can be felt at the top. That movement can be troublesome in some situations. The upper storeys of the former Twin Towers in New York, for example, were always evacuated in a storm. People working in one tower could feel their own tower shaking and see the other tower swaying. That was not a pleasant experience.

On land, damper systems are nothing new. These days, many skyscrapers have been made vibration-proof to increase comfort. That can

be achieved, for example, by adding shock absorbers. In that case, a pendulum, weight or fluid at the top of the building acts as a brake. If the building wants to move in one direction, the brake moves it the other way, sometimes automatically. The 508-m-high Taipei 101 in Taiwan for instance, uses a 'tuned mass damper' in the form of a gold coloured ball weighing 800 tons. The ball works by moving in the opposite direction from the tower, which slows down the movement.

This facility has become standard by now, but in Japan they go one step further. Many buildings on dry land there are supported by a foundation containing steel springs, to counteract the effects of an earthquake. The Shiodome Sumitomo Building in Tokyo for example, consists of two parts. The upper part of the building, with 16 storeys and 49,100 tons approximately two-thirds of the total weight, is seismically isolated from the lower 11 storeys. Between the eleventh and twelfth storey there is a sort of crawl space with seismic insulation. The top 16 storeys are supported by 41 rubber columns, 14 steel springs and 100 massive lead pipes, which are underpinned by the ceiling of the eleventh floor. They ensure that the upper part of the building can move freely in a horizontal direction in the event of an earthquake. If the upper part has shifted in relation to the lower part after an earthquake, there are yellow ridges

The tuned mass demper in Taipei 101.

The upper part of the Shiodome Sumitomo building in Tokyo is seismically isolated from the lower 11 storeys. The top 16 storeys are supported by 41 rubber columns, 14 steel springs and 100 massive lead pipes. They ensure that the upper part of the building can move freely in a horizontal direction in the event of an earthquake.

where a jack can be inserted to put the top 16 storeys back into place. These sorts of technological innovations ensure that in regions where the risk of earthquakes is high – previously unsuitable for high-rise – tall structures can now be built.[52]

The same sort of technological renewal is needed for building on water. The solution for dynamic stabilization of floating buildings lies in the area of mass transference in the buoyant construction, to compensate for the water swell. The technology works on the same principle as the tuned mass damper in a skyscraper. If a wave comes along, a weight moves to the place where the wave is building up, so that the platform remains stable. Particularly in a location with a dominant or one-sided wave direction, it is possible to stabilize the foundations by tuning the frequency of the mass damper to the frequency of the waves. Static dampers, in the form of hydraulic systems or spring systems are already being applied for this purpose, too. So the threat lies not so much in the technical feasibility of the desired level of comfort, but in the financial consequences of the shock absorption systems. Significant innovative progress can still be made here.

A SWOT analysis gives a picture of the current state of play in an upcoming market. If the threats and weaknesses clearly have the upper hand on the strengths and opportunities, that can be an indication that the market does not have momentum yet. However, that is not the case with living on water. There are certainly threats, but the realization of a few prominent break-through projects can establish the feasibility and desirability without a shadow of a doubt. Examples are The New Water project in the Netherlands and the floating islands in the Maldives, both of which are being carried out in public-private partnerships with the local authorities. The realization of these projects also achieves a reduction in the weaknesses. In this case, the weaknesses relate mainly to the fact that the opportunities have not yet been realized. Living on water has reached a sufficiently critical mass for the go-ahead to be given for the next development phase, in which floating buildings in both perception and reality are the equal of buildings on land.

A New Generation of Designers

Global brainers are already busy on the Internet, dreaming up solutions for the threats and weaknesses. They are doing that from the conviction that they have influence on the world around them, and that they can make that world a better place. It would be a good thing if this sort of enterprising mentality were taught at the universities, instead of endless studies of form and other noncommittal subjects.

In the last decades, students have grown up with the idea that architecture is all about building a statement. In this vision, the most important contribution you can make to society is to establish a monument for yourself, in the shape of a gigantic building carrying your signature. Lately, starchitects have been more concerned with the design of an object and

'I WANT TO END THE CURRENT PHASE OF ARCHITECTURAL IDOLATRY – THE AGE OF THE ICON' REM KOOLHAAS

with their own ego than with finding solutions to social problems. The generation of architects now acquiring fame is between 30 and 40 years old and grew up with the idols of the previous generation. Koolhaas, Gehry, Calatrava: those were the architects of the icon and the grand gesture. They made buildings as products, completely in the modernist tradition, detached from urban relevance or local culture. Gehry's museum in Bilbao may have provided economic growth for the city – of which every mayor in the world is jealous – but it is chiefly a work of art that has got nothing to do with solving contemporary problems – and is not suitable for exhibiting other works of art either, according to many critics.

Koolhaas, always on the leading edge, was the first architect who began to find this position uncomfortable, when he sent in his competition design 'Dubai Renaissance' for a building in the Emirate of the same name in 2006. He proposed an 'anti-icon': a white box completely lacking in identity. 'The ambition of this project is to end the current phase of architectural idolatry – the age of the icon – where obsession with individual genius far exceeds commitment to the collective effort that is needed to construct the city,' wrote Koolhaas in his explanation. 'So far, the 21st century trend in city building leads to a mad and meaningless overdose of themes, extremes, egos and extravagance.'

It is most certainly time for a different approach. Students should be taught to realize that another world begins with them; that they carry responsibility for thinking about ways in which a society can function better in an alternative way.

The established order of clients, developers, builders and architects is generally not in the least interested in dreaming about a better future, at any rate if it goes any further than a few pictures and words without obligations. Because then they would have to put their career on the line, throw security overboard and step into a market they think is full of all sorts of dangers. But it could also be different, as the Dutch urban designer Ashok Bhalotra demonstrates. 'One who does not dare to dream, is not a realist,' is one of his well-known statements. In March 2010, aged 67, he decided to dedicate himself to a better world, from his professional

The Guggenheim museum in Bilbao, Spain, designed by Frank Gehry, is a work of art in its own right.

In 2006, Rem Koolhaas
protested against
'the current phase of
architectural idolatry'
and 'the obsession with
individual genius' with his
design Dubai Renaissance.

position. He left the large architecture firm he directed and
founded FEWS for more. He wants to try to provide more
people with Food, Energy, Water and Shelter through this
organization. A drastic decision like this is only possible if
you are prepared to let go of existing certainties. It can be
done when you are 67, but also when you are 47 or 27.

Journalist Tracy Metz once set this caption above her
article on the work of Waterstudio: 'Save the world, build
on water!' The heading was not entirely free of sarcasm, but
is not untrue either: you really can change the world with
floating buildings.[53]

Building on water can contribute to finding solutions
to a large number of problems: protection against flooding
in Bangladesh, water and energy facilities in China, better
foundation technology in the Netherlands, autonomous food
production on the Maldives, space in Tokyo and sustainability
in the UAE. Rising sea levels, urbanization and the corresponding lack of space have created momentum for building
on water. These threats to prosperity provide architects with
a platform on which to express themselves. But they really do

Study by Waterstudio for
a floating city near Malé
in the Maldives. The city
consists of a large number
of interlinked components.
Transport takes place
mainly over water.

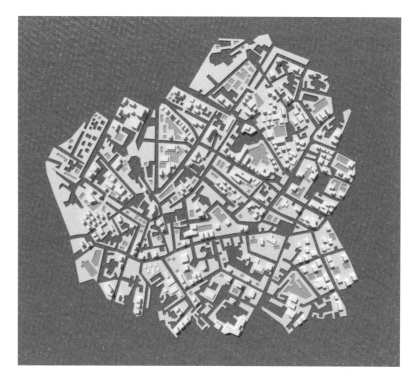

need to grasp the opportunity. Building on water has changed in the last few years due to differentiation of urban construction from an exclusive type of housing for privileged people only to a self-evident intervention to improve the living environment for large groups of people. These improvements are not the same for every location, but can be achieved at any location on water.

Architects, builders, developers and manufacturers of the climate-change generation will only be able to realize socially and economically relevant projects if they take a new look at spatial structure, in which water plays an essential role. *Float!* brings an additional clear message: build on water. This single syllable sounds like a simple exclamation, but there is a world of possibilities hidden behind the five letters. FLOAT is an acronym that stands for Flexible Land On Aquatic Territory. Urban development on floating foundations creates an unprecedented flexibility on water, which increases the possibilities for planning for change.

If the designers and builders of the climate-change generation want to alter anything, they must not look at the limitations but at the opportunities. The momentum for building on water is present. In other words: let your imagination drift and let your creativity *Float*!

INDEX

Index

PEOPLE, PLACES & PHENOMENA

3ds Max: *280*
Aalsmeer: *60*
Aboriginals: *221*
Abu Dhabi: *221*
Adriatic Sea: *124, 234, 235*
Afsluitdijk: *156, 160*
Al Al-Shaali, Rashed: *213*
Alabama: *244*
Albania: *179*
Alexandria: *117*
Alkmaar: *76*
Allseas Marine Contractors: *245*
Almere: *238, 253*
Al-Sallal, Khaled: *213*
Amfora: *85, 86, 87*
Amstel River: *122*
Amsterdam: *22, 29, 36, 44, 46,
    47, 50, 59, 63, 64, 65, 67, 85,
    86, 87, 90, 122, 123, 124, 136,
    142, 143, 144, 149, 150, 151,
    152, 157, 180, 181, 183, 184,
    185, 276, 277, 285*
Amur River: *192*
An Inconvenient Truth: *5, 204, 205*
Anarchism: *28*
Antarctica: *191*
Antigua and Barbados: *252*
Anti-icon: *290*
Antwerp: *22, 115, 116*
Apollo 13: *244*
Apple: *265, 266*
Aquapolis: *273, 276*
Arabian Gulf: *215*
Arcadis: *181*
Archigram: *267, 270, 271, 272*
Archipelago cities: *115, 123, 124,
    125, 128, 133*
Architecture blogs: *279*
Argentina: *58*
Arnhem: *239*

ARO: *134*
Arup: *54*
Atelier de Lyon: *184, 185*
Australia: *206, 212, 221*
Aztecs: *125, 126*
B-15 Ice Floe: *191*
Bacardi: *222*
Bajau Laut: *194*
Bangkok: *115, 118, 119, 120, 124*
Bangladesh: *196, 197, 291*
Barcelona chair: *74*
Barcelona: *37, 117, 192*
Barceloneta Beach: *192*
Bates, Michael: *234*
Bates, Roy: *223, 234, 235, 249*
Bay of Bengal: *196*
Beemster: *75*
Beijing: *31, 32, 33, 37*
Benz, Carl: *284*
Berlin: *19, 26, 30, 193*
Beyond the waterfront: *68, 88*
Bhalotra, Ashok: *290*
Bijnkershoek, Cornelis van: *247*
Bilbao: *289, 290*
Bini Systems: *80*
Biogrout: *194*
Birma: *197*
Black Madonna: *208, 209*
Blade Runner: *80*
Bolivia: *179*
Bombay: *55, 96, 97*
Bondi Beach: *192*
Boston: *22, 135, 271, 273*
BP: *243, 244, 245*
Brasilia: *17*
Braungart, Michael: *205*
Brindley, Lynne: *263*
British Library: *263*
Bruges: *122*
Brussels: *22*

Buckminster Fuller, Richard: *267,
    270, 271, 272, 274, 276*
Buddhism: *58*
Buenos Aires: *117, 118*
Bueren, Bart van: *240*
Building for Change: *17*
Building on Floating Landscapes: *179*
Buoyant concrete: *89*
Buoyant foundation: *6, 62, 88, 89,
    105, 283, 285*
Burj Khalifa: *30, 79, 80*
Burning Man: *36*
Bushmen: *221*
Bushnell, Dennis: *189*
Cabotage: *252, 253*
Cairo: *118*
Calatrava, Santiago: *8, 289*
Calcutta: *196*
Camp, Paul van de: *6*
Canada: *249, 253*
Canal cities: *115, 122, 124*
Cancún: *175, 176, 178*
Cape Town: *117, 192*
Capitol: *74*
Carbon-free footprint: *221*
CCTV tower: *31*
Central Park: *65, 181*
Centre Suisse d'Electronique et
    de Microtechnique: *101*
Chalk, Warren: *270, 272*
Chao Phraya River: *119, 120*
Cheonggyecheon River: *118,
    119, 129*
Chilingarov, Artur: *248, 249*
China: *31, 32, 58, 67, 98, 125,
    159, 183, 188, 249, 291*
Cincinnati: *118*
City farming: *57*
Class system: *27*
Cleveland: *189*

Clifton Beach: *192*
Climate change generation: *19*
Closing the gap: *49*
Club of Rome: *207*
Codex Leicester: *262, 263, 264, 267*
Commission on the Limits of the
    Continental Shelf: *249*
Communism: *28, 30*
Condamine Harbour: *92*
Conservatism: *28*
Consumption urbanism: *9, 67*
Continental shelf submissions:
    248, 249, 253
Copacabana Beach: *192*
Copenhagen: *206*
Coral bleaching: *211, 212*
Corneliszoon, Cornelis: *76, 77*
Corporatism: *28*
Cradle to Cradle: *205, 221*
Cramer, Jacqueline: *239*
Crystal Palace: *78*
Dam Square: *50*
DARPA: *95*
De Jure Praedae: *246*
Dead Sea: *192*
Deepwater Horizon: *243, 244*
Defence Line of Amsterdam:
    151, 152
Delft Hydraulics: *159*
Delft University of Technology:
    147, 224
Delft: *36, 246*
Delta Works: *154, 155, 156, 160*
Deltares: *160, 194, 245*
DeltaSync: *240*
Den Helder: *242*
Denmark: *178, 249*
Depolderization: *7, 8, 161, 162,
    163, 166*
Desalination: *98, 192*
Dike Board: *152*
Dike Reeve: *152, 153*
Discovery Channel: *5, 45, 80, 81*
District Water Board: *8, 148,
    152, 154*
Double-decker city: *82, 84*
Drygalski Ice Tongue: *191*
Dubai: *6, 8, 9, 30, 32, 34, 52, 54,
    79, 190, 192, 193, 194, 215, 224,
    290, 291*
Dublin: *64*
Dura Vermeer: *58, 59, 188*
Dutch Docklands: *6, 7, 9, 61, 89,
    186, 187, 188, 191, 192, 194,
    195, 277*
Dutch East India Company: *76, 123,
    144, 246*
Dutch Municipalities Bank: *8, 163*
Dutch War of Independence: *151*
Dutch West India Company: *76, 123*
Dynamic cities: *9, 65, 136*
Dynamic stabilization: *288*
Earls Court: *205*
Earthquake: *91, 126, 148, 287, 288*
Eastern Scheldt flood barrier: *156*
Ecobuild fair: *205*
École Militaire: *73*
Ecologism: *28*
Economic change: *31*
EDAW: *37*
Eiffel Tower: *72, 73, 74, 78*
Ellis Island: *173*
Elschot, Willem: *75*
Empire State Building: *74, 78*
England: *76, 123*
Eskimos: *114, 221*
Evergreen Point Floating Bridge: *92*
Exclusive Economic Zone: *248, 250*
Exodus, or the Voluntary Prisoners
    of Architecture: *19*
Expanding the urban fabric: *9, 62,
    63, 64*
Expo 75: *273, 276*
Extreme Engineering: *80, 81*

Exxon Mobil: *244, 245*
Eyjafjallajökull volcano: *277, 278*
Facebook: *32, 242, 266*
Falangism: *28*
Fascism: *28*
Fens: *178, 179*
FEWS for more: *291*
Filled polder: *161, 162*
First World War: *151, 247*
Flatiron Building: *78*
Flevoland: *156, 157, 160*
Flexible buildings: *59, 208*
Floating agriculture: *58, 103,
    188, 238*
Floating airport: *91*
Floating apartment complex: *7, 9*
Floating beaches: *7, 192, 194, 213*
Floating cruise ship terminal: *7*
Floating farming: *190*
Floating food: *188*
Floating foundation: *48, 49, 50,
    51, 57, 88, 89, 91, 128, 174,
    210, 292*
Floating fresh water: *190, 192*
Floating golf course: *9, 186, 187*
Floating green: *179, 181, 183, 186*
Floating greenhouse: *58, 59, 188*
Floating high-rise building: *54,
    64, 91*
Floating ice floe: *190, 191*
Floating landscapes: *173, 174, 178,
    179, 183, 184, 188, 198*
Floating mosque: *7, 215, 216, 218*
Floating office building: *90*
Floating parking garage: *92, 130*
Floating pavilion: *240, 241*
Floating prison: *91*
Floating road: *92, 97, 283*
Floating safe zones: *194*
Floating solar blanket: *101, 102*
Floating tower: *7*
Flooding risk: *157*
Flores: *125*
Florida, Richard: *21, 22, 24, 135*
Florida: *244*
France: *178*
Franco-Prussian War: *151*
Freak architecture: *284*
Free waters: *246*
Freedom of the Seas: *235, 246, 247,
    248, 249*
Friction pile foundation: *51*
Friedman, Patri: *235*
Fugro: *245*
Future on water: *45*
Gates, Bill: *113, 263, 264, 266, 267*
Gaynor, John P.: *78*
Gehry, Frank: *289, 290*
General Motors: *132*
Genghis Khan: *31*
Germany: *19, 26, 67, 154, 155,
    159, 178*
Gibraltar: *97*
Giesen, Marleen van: *8*
Glenn Research Center: *189*
Global brain: *281, 289*
Google Buzz: *242*
Gore, Al: *5, 204, 205*
Gouda: *50, 148*
Governors Island: *133, 173*
Gramlich, Wayne: *235*
Great Barrier Reef: *212*
Great Britain: *95, 121, 175*
Great Pacific Garbage Patch: *103*
Great Pyramid at Giza: *80*
Greenland: *249, 254*
Greenpeace: *225*
Greyhound: *132*
Groot, Hugo de: *246, 247*
Grootveld, Robert Jasper: *184*
Guangzhou: *118*
Guatemala: *125*
Gulf of Mexico: *243, 244, 245*
Haarlem: *50, 150*

Haarlemmermeer Polder: *150, 154,
    155, 158*
Hadid, Zaha: *8*
Hamburg: *64, 115, 116*
Hampton: *189*
Han River: *61, 62, 118, 129*
Haughwout Building: *78*
Hausmann, Georges Eugène Baron: *29*
Hawaii: *103*
Hazra, Sugata: *196, 197*
Heat stress: *182*
Heemskerk, Admiral Jacob van: *246*
Helsinki: *123*
Hendricks, Robert: *189*
Henry Hudson Parkway: *64*
Hertogin Hedwige Polder: *161*
Herzog & De Meuron: *37*
Heyerdahl, Thor: *267*
Hidayati, Nur: *225*
Hinderling, Thomas: *101*
Hirata, Akihisa: *279*
Ho Chi Minh: *63, 118*
Holland America Line: *239*
Holtrop, Anne: *186*
Hong Kong: *55, 124, 125*
Hoofddorp: *150*
Hoover Dam: *135*
Hornby Vellard: *123*
Houston: *84, 85*
Houthavens: *90*
Hudson River: *64, 133*
Hulhumalé: *188*
Hurricane Emily: *176, 178*
Hurricane Katrina: *19*
Hutong: *31, 32*
Hyde Park: *181*
Hydraulic system: *288*
Hydrocity: *113, 127, 128, 129, 131,
    133, 136*
Iceland: *277, 278*
Icon: *289, 290*
IJ River: *184, 185, 186*
IJburg: *44, 45, 46, 47, 185, 186,
    276, 277*
IJsselmeer: *142, 149, 156*
Impulses for change: *25*
India: *98, 126, 158, 159, 196,
    247, 249*
Indian Ocean: *126, 127, 186*
Individualism: *19*
Indonesia: *159, 194, 224, 225, 226*
Inle Lake: *197*
Intergovernmental Panel on Climate
    Change: *206*
Inundation: *151*
iPhone: *265, 266*
iPod: *266*
Isla Mujeres: *176, 178*
Islam: *58*
Islamism: *28*
Island cities: *115, 125, 133*
Islay Island: *101*
Israel: *192*
Italy: *178*
Jadavpur University: *196*
Jamaica: *191*
Japan: *80, 81, 91, 103, 148, 271, 273,
    276, 287*
JDS: *54, 56*
Jobs, Steve: *265, 266*
Jordan: *192*
Jumsai, Sumet: *267*
Kaafu Atoll: *126, 129*
Kalimantan: *159*
Kansai International Airport: *91*
Karimun Islands: *225*
Kazakhstan: *188*
Keuning, David: *9*
Khlong: *119, 120*
Kikutake, Kiyonori: *270, 272,
    273, 276*
Knock John Tower: *233*
KNSM: *63, 90, 184*
Kollhoff, Hans: *208, 209*

Koolhaas, Rem: *8, 19, 289, 290, 291*
Kowloon peninsula: *125*
Krung Thep: *119*
Laguna Veneta: *124*
Lake Washington: *92*
Langley Research Center: *189*
Le Corbusier: *74, 284*
League of Nations: *247*
Leblanc, Patrick: *186*
LEED certification system: *19*
Leeghwater, Jan Adriaanszoon:
    75, 76, 77
Legatum: *22, 23*
Leiden: *150, 151, 246*
Lena River: *192*
Leninism: *28*
Leonardo da Vinci: *262, 263, 264,*
    267, 281
Liberalism: *28*
Liberty Island: *173*
Listing: *286*
Liverpool: *64*
Lomonosov Reef: *249, 254*
London: *37, 63, 65, 67, 82, 83, 118,*
    121, 131, 136, 181, 205, 207,
    213, 263, 272
Long Island: *133*
Louis XIII, King: *180*
Louisiana: *244*
LTL Architects: *134*
Maas Harbour: *240*
Maeslandt flood barrier: *156*
Make It Right foundation: *19, 20*
Malaysia: *194, 195, 224, 225*
Maldives: *9, 125, 126, 127, 129,*
    186, 187, 211, 212, 254, 288,
    291, 292
Malé: *125, 126, 129, 187, 188*
Malta: *222*
Mammoet van Seumeren: *91*
Mammoet: *245*
Manhattan Transcripts: *19*
Manhattan: *55, 64, 65, 133, 135,*
    136, 254
Maoism: *28*
Mare Liberum: *246, 247*
Markarfljöt River: *278*
Marxism: *28*
Mass transference: *288*
Matthew Baird Architects: *134*
Maunsell Sea Forts: *95, 233*
Maya: *280*
Mazdar City: *221*
McDonough, William: *205*
Medici, Maria de: *180, 181*
Mega-Float consortium: *91*
Mega-region: *22*
Mersey River: *95*
Metabolists: *270*
Metz, Tracy: *291*
Meuse River: *143*
Mexcaltitan: *125*
Mexico City: *98*
Mexico: *125, 126, 175*
Meyer, Han: *224*
Mi-8 attack helicopter: *191*
Microsoft: *113, 263, 264*
Middle Ages: *51, 122*
Middle East: *98, 188, 190, 221*
Mies van der Rohe, Ludwig: *74*
Mitsubishi Heavy Industries: *91*
Modernism: *18*
Momentum: *263, 264, 267, 268, 276,*
    279, 288, 291, 292
Monaco: *55, 92*
Mongolia: *220, 221*
Monier, Joseph: *88*
Montenegro: *179*
Montreal: *84, 85*
Moore, Charles: *103*
Moore, Jack: *234*
Morocco: *97*
Morphosis: *20, 29*
Moveable cities: *67, 68*

Muiden: *151*
Mumbai: *117, 123*
MVRDV: *102*
Myanmar: *197*
Myung Bak, Lee: *119, 129*
Naaldwijk: *58, 188*
Naarden: *151*
Nakheel: *7*
Nanjing: *118*
Napoleon III, Emporer: *29*
nARCHITECTS: *134*
NASA: *189*
Nasheed, Mohamed, *9, 127*
National Geographic: *134*
Nationalism: *28*
Natural Floating Landscapes: *178*
Nautilus: *183*
Nayarit coastal marshes: *125*
Netherlands Architecture Institute:
    184
Netherlands: *5, 7, 8, 27, 45, 46, 48,*
    49, 50, 51, 58, 59, 60, 63, 68,
    75, 76, 77, 78, 85, 91, 96, 100,
    142, 143, 144, 145, 146, 147,
    148, 149, 151, 152, 153, 154,
    155, 156, 157, 158, 159, 160,
    161, 162, 166, 178, 179, 188,
    194, 197, 207, 221, 245, 254,
    276, 288, 291
Nevada: *36*
New Amsterdam: *64*
New density: *24, 25, 283*
New Dutch Waterline: *151*
New flexibility: *32, 283*
New Guinea: *221*
New Moore Island: *196*
New Orleans: *5*
New Water Movement: *160, 161*
New York: *22, 55, 64, 65, 67, 78,*
    91, 131, 133, 134, 135, 136, 173,
    181, 286
New Zealand: *191*
Next World: *45*
Niemeyer, Oscar: *17, 18, 38, 16*
Nieuwerkerk: *145, 150*
Nieuw-Vennep: *144, 150*
Nipah Island: *225*
Non-rigids: *174*
Noordoostpolder: *156, 157*
North Pole: *221*
North Sea: *99, 100, 143, 146, 154,*
    155, 156, 158, 160, 232, 233,
    242, 243, 248, 249
Norway: *99, 190, 191, 249*
Nouvel, Jean: *8*
O'Rahilly, Ronan: *234*
Oasis of the Seas: *93, 94*
Ob River: *191*
Off-shore industries: *55*
Ohio: *189*
Oil platform: *54, 94, 100, 236*
Okinawa: *273, 276*
Olthuis, Koen: *4, 5, 6, 7, 8, 9*
Olympic Games: *37, 38, 121*
OMA: *100*
Online media: *279, 280*
Orang Laut: *194*
Osaka: *91*
Oscillating water column: *101*
Otis, Elisha: *78, 82*
Oude Essink, Gualbert: *160*
Pacific Ocean: *94, 103, 104*
Palace of Westminster: *74*
Palm Jumeirah: *223, 224*
Pampus Plan: *276*
Paraná River,: *117, 118*
Parc du Champs de Mars: *73*
Paris Plages: *193*
Paris: *29, 30, 72, 73, 74, 118, 193*
Patent-Motorwagen: *284*
PayPal: *235*
Pentagon: *95*
Pentecostal church: *58, 59*
Peru: *179*

Peten Itza Lake: *125*
Peters, Rolf: *4*
Philadelphia: *118*
Phillipines: *194*
Pig City: *102*
Pile foundation: *49, 50, 51, 129, 283*
Pitt, Brad: *19*
Plattenbau: *30*
Poel Polder: *162*
Poland: *178*
Polder as water column: *161, 162*
Polder model: *151, 152*
Political change: *28*
Port cities: *115, 130*
Portugal: *246, 254*
Pragmatism: *28*
Princess Amalia Wind Farm: *99*
PTW: *37*
Public Domain Architects: *240*
Puerto Aventuras: *175*
Purmer: *75*
Pyramid City: *80*
Queensland: *212*
Raisbeck, Peter: *270*
Randstad: *146, 160*
Ras al Khaimah Emirate: *101*
Rashid Al Maktoum, Emir Sheikh
    Mohammed bin: *32*
Rashid al Maktoum,
    Sjeik Mohammed bin: *7*
Razee, Mahmood: *186*
Republic of Seven United
    Netherlands: *77*
Rhine Harbour: *240*
Rhine River: *117, 143*
Rhino: *280*
Riau: *225*
Rietveld Landscape: *184, 185*
Rijk: *150*
Rimini: *234, 235*
Rio de Janeiro: *17, 38, 116, 117, 192*
Rio de la Plata, *117, 118*
River cities: *115, 118, 119, 121, 133*
Roman Catholic Church: *144*
Rome: *136, 279*
Rosa, Giorgio: *234, 235, 249*
Rose Island: *235*
Ross Ice Shelf: *191*
Rotterdam: *19, 64, 91, 115, 116, 117,*
    130, 131, 150, 153, 157, 193,
    223, 239, 240
Rotting peat landscape: *158*
Rougerie, Jacques: *267, 270*
Roughs Tower: *234*
Royal Boskalis Westminster: *245*
Royal Caribbean International:
    93, 94
Royal Haskoning: *7, 91*
Russell, Peter: *281*
Russia: *99, 100, 158, 248, 259, 253, 254*
Rybinsk reservoir: *179*
Saline agriculture: *189, 190*
Saline seepage: *158, 160, 162, 189*
Salinization: *160*
Salsette: *123*
Sand war: *224*
Santa Catarina: *246*
Sapir, Edward: *114*
Sassen, Saskia: *24*
Sauer, Frank: *190*
SBM Offshore: *245*
SCAPE: *134*
Scarless developments: *9, 220, 221,*
    225, 226
Scenario for the next 100 years: *51*
Schiedam: *91*
Schiphol Airport: *150, 160*
Sealand: *232, 233, 234*
Seasteading Institute: *235, 236,*
    237, 249
Seattle: *92*
Second World War: *18, 27, 30, 95,*
    151, 265
Seine River: *192, 193*

Semi-rigids: *174*
Semi-submersible: *94, 97, 98*
Seoul: *55, 61, 118, 119, 129, 130*
Shan Hills: *197*
Shanghai: *276*
Shell: *244, 245*
Shenzhen: *19*
Shimizu corporation: *80*
Shimizu Mega-City Pyramid: *80*
Shiodome Sumitomo Building: *287, 288*
Shock absorbers: *287, 288*
Siege of Leiden: *151*
Silicon Valley: *67*
Singapore: *55, 224, 225, 226*
Sinking land: *158*
Skadar Lake: *179*
Sketchup: *280*
Sky City 1000: *81, 82*
Skyscraper: *78, 79, 80, 81, 82, 135, 286, 288*
Smit International: *245*
Snug Harbor: *173*
Social change: *18, 26, 27, 58, 242*
Social networks: *27, 32, 33, 242, 279, 280*
Socialism: *28*
Solar energy: *98, 100, 101, 102, 103, 219*
Somerset Levels: *178*
Soons, Fred: *247*
South Holland: *154, 156, 157, 163, 165*
South Korea: *61*
South Talpatti Island: *196*
Sowa, Rishi: *175, 176, 178*
Spain: *74, 76, 92, 123, 151, 234, 246, 247, 254*
Speer, Albert: *30*
Spiral Island: *175, 176, 178*
Spread foundation: *50*
Spring system: *288*
Sri Lanka: *9, 127, 254*
SS Rotterdam: *239, 240, 253*
Stability: *97, 103, 286*
Stalinism: *28*
Starchitects: *289*
Staten Island: *133*
Static damper: *288*
Stockholm: *123, 124*
Strukton: *85, 87*
Student protests: *19*
Studio Noach: *186*
Sukhoi fighter jet: *191*
Sumatra: *159*
Sumitomo Heavy Industries: *91*
Sunderban delta: *196, 197*

Sustainability: *205, 206, 207, 208, 209, 219, 226, 291*
Sustainaquality: *208, 209, 219, 226, 205*
SWOT: *281, 288*
Sydney: *117, 118, 192*
Taipei *101: 287*
Taiwan: *287*
Takenaka corporation: *81*
Tange, Kenzo: *270, 271, 273, 276*
Tavistock Square: *83*
Technological change: *30*
Technology leap: *73*
Tenochtitlan: *125, 126*
Tension-leg platform: *94*
Territorial waters: *233, 246, 247, 248, 249, 254*
Texas: *244*
Texcoco Lake: *125, 126*
Thames Barrier: *121*
Thames Gateway: *63, 121*
Thames River: *37, 63, 83, 95, 121*
The floating Dutchman: *4, 5*
The Hague: *153, 157, 208, 209, 247*
The New Water: *8, 63, 162, 163, 165, 166, 288*
The World: *224*
Thiel, Peter: *235*
Thon Buri: *120*
Tiananmen Square: *33*
Timaru: *191*
Titanic: *93, 94*
Titicaca Lake: *179, 180*
Tokyo: *80, 81, 92, 117, 131, 271, 273, 274, 276, 279, 287, 288, 291*
Trading places: *9, 55, 57, 58, 59, 61, 62*
Traditionalism: *18*
Tromsø: *190, 191*
Tschumi, Bernard: *19*
Tsunami: *5, 126, 187, 197, 278*
Tuned mass damper: *287, 288*
Twelve Years' Truce: *247*
Twin Towers: *286*
Twitter: *32, 33, 242, 266*
Typhoon: *148*
UAE: *30, 35, 101, 190, 219, 221, 222, 223, 224, 291*
Uitgeest: *76*
Ukraine: *99*
UMTS: *241*
UN Convention on the Law of the Sea: *247, 248*
United Arab Emirates University: *213*
United Nations: *247, 249*
Urban heat islands: *213*

Uros Indians: *179, 180*
Uruguay River: *117, 118*
USA: *30, 36, 67, 102, 104, 112, 131, 132, 159, 204, 244, 249, 253, 254, 265, 273*
Utrecht: *146, 147, 151*
Uzbekistan: *188*
Van den Broek & Bakema: *276*
Van Oord: *223, 224, 245*
Vancouver: *117, 118*
Venice: *19, 119, 123, 124, 128, 132, 133*
Vernon C. Bain Center: *91*
Vijfhuizen: *150*
Virginia: *189*
Visualization technologies: *279*
Vondel Park: *181*
Voorburg, Arie: *181, 182*
Vulnerable society: *277*
Waal River: *143*
Washington: *22, 135*
Wasterdyk Vermuyden, Cornelius: *178*
Water Control Board: *163*
Waterfront cities: *115, 116, 117, 118, 123*
Waterstudio: *4, 5, 7, 8, 45, 46, 48, 52, 54, 58, 59, 60, 62, 134, 162, 186, 187, 190, 191, 192, 215, 291, 292*
Wave energy: *100*
Wave frequency: *286, 288*
Weeber, Carel: *208, 209*
Weesp: *151*
Weijden, Roderick van der: *186*
Westland: *153, 162, 163, 165*
Wet polder: *115, 161, 162*
Wetlands International: *159*
Whorf, Benjamin Lee: *114*
Willem I, King: *150, 151*
Wilnis: *147*
Wilson, Woodrow: *247*
Wind power: *100*
Windows Vista: *263*
Woolworth Building: *78*
World Bank: *98*
Yamaichi, Hachiro: *91*
Yellow Coach: *132*
Yenisey River: *192*
Young & Rubicam: *222*
Zaandam: *91*
Zeekracht: *100*
Zeeland: *154, 156, 157, 161*
Zuiderzee: *156*
Zuidplas Polder: *148*
Zwarts & Jansma: *85, 87*

CREDITS

Credits

FOOTNOTES

1　'Brazil's 102-year-old architect spends 'crap' birthday', AFP, 15 December 2009

2　Richard Florida, Tim Gulden, Charlotta Mellander, *The Rise of the Mega-Region*, The Martin Prosperity Institute, October 2007

3　www.prosperity.com

4　'Amsterdam Make-Over 2040', *Tegenlicht*, VPRO, 14 September 2009

5　Henk Leenaers, 'Stedelijk Waterbeheer in Dordrecht en Delft – Grondwater zorgt voor problemen', *TNO Magazine*, September 2006

6　Bina Venkataraman, 'Country, the City Version: Farms in the Sky Gain New Interest', *New York Times*, 15 July 2008

7　Nicolas Geyrhalter, *Our Daily Bread*, 2006

8　Elke Beyer, Anke Hagemann, Tim Rieniets, Philipp Oswalt, *Atlas of Shrinking Cities*, Hatje Cantz Publishers, June 2006

9　George H. Douglas, *Skyscrapers: A Social History of the Very Tall Building in America*, McFarland & Company, August 2004

10　Paul Murphy, Intelligence and Security Committee, *Report into the London Terrorist Attacks on 7 July 2005*, Presented to Parliament by the Prime Minister by Command of Her Majesty, May 2006

11　www.bontezwaan.nl

12　Lewis Page, 'US Navy plans self-building floating fortresses', *The Register*, 24 March 2010

13　Michael Krebs, 'Water shortage in Mexico City could echo the global water issue', *Digital Journal*, 27 September 2009

14　Alexis Madrigal, 'Researcher Pushes Enormous Floating Solar Islands', *Wired*, 20 May 2008. See also www.solar-islands.com

15　See www.verticalfarm.com and www.eco-tower.com

16　Kathy Marks and Daniel Howden, 'The world's rubbish dump: a tip that stretches from Hawaii to Japan', *The Independent*, 5 February 2008

17　Herman Algra a.o., *Actieplan slimme en schone stedelijke distributie Amsterdam*, Dienst Infrastructuur Verkeer en Vervoer, Gemeente Amsterdam, February 2010

18　See www.ahn.nl/postcodetool

19　For extensive information about the New Dutch Waterline, see Rita Brons and Bernard Colenbrander, *Atlas of the New Dutch Water Defence Line*, 010 Publishers, 2009. See also www. hollandsewaterlinie.nl

20　Michael Persson, 'Indonesisch veen draagt sterk bij aan opwarming', *de Volkskrant*, 3 November 2006

21　Eric le Gras, 'Het grondwater in Nederland verzilt', *Trouw*, 16 March 2005

22　See www.spiralislanders.com

23　'Hoog bezoek!', *Anno*, Museum of National History, 31 March 2009

24　Barbara Sanders, 'Hittestress verlamt grote stad', *De Financiële Telegraaf*, 15 December 2009

25　Judith Evans, 'Floating golf course where you can really sink a putt', *The Times*, 2 April 2010

26　See www.blue-crystal.de

27　Ayinde O. Chase, 'Russian Military Set To Bomb Ice-

Clogged Rivers To Prevent Flooding', *All Headline News*, 24 March 2010

28   'Disputed Bay of Bengal island 'vanishes' say scientists', *BBC News*, 24 March 2010

29   Jos Lichtenberg, *Slim Bouwen*, Aeneas, 2005

30   Maarten Keulemans, 'Zandtaartjes boven de zeespiegel', *Delta*, 23 June 2005

31   Jacco Neleman, 'Arabisch Baggerparadijs', *FEM Business* , volume 8, number 17, 30 April 2005

32   Barney Henderson, 'Singapore accused of launching 'Sand Wars', *Telegraph*, 12 February 2010

33   See www.sealandnews.com and www.sealandgov.org

34   See http://rose-island. livenations.net

35   For even more attempts at establishing micronations, see Erwin S. Strauss, *How to Start Your Own Country*, Breakout Productions, February 1984 and John Ryan, George Dunford and Simon Sellars, *Micronations: The Lonely Planet Guide to Home-Made Nations*, Lonely Planet, 1 September 2006

36   Shelby Erdman, 'City floating on the sea could be just 3 years away', *CNN*, 10 March 2009 and Alexis Madrigal, 'Peter Thiel makes down payment on libertarian ocean colonies', *Wired*, 19 May 2008

37   Verdict LJN BB6079, Arnhem Court of Justice, nr. 06/00491, 15 October 2007 and verdict

LJN BK9136, Supreme Court of the Netherlands, nr. 07/13305, 15 January 2010

38   Jan Jager, 'Arrest Hoge Raad: Drijvend bouwen op losse schroeven?', *Water Wonen & Ruimte*, volume 3, issue 02, 2010

39   Tim Webb, 'BP boss admits job on the line over Gulf oil spill', *The Guardian*, 14 May 2010 and Terry Macalister, 'BP admits blame for Texas oil disaster', *The Guardian*, 18 May 2005

40   Kees Versluis, 'Olieplatforms, de feiten', *Intermediair*, 6 May 2010

41   Yasuaki Onuma, 'Hugo Grotius', *Encyclopædia Britannica*

42   Folkert Jensma, 'Grotius' vrije zee raakt uit gratie', *NRC Handelsblad*, 12 December 2009. For a full, online facsimile of *Mare Liberum*, see www.kb.nl/galerie/mareliberum

43   Theo Deutinger, 'Exclusive Economic Zone', *Mark – Another Architecture*, issue 22, October / November 2009

44   'Russische vlag 'wappert' onder de Noordpool', *de Volkskrant*, 3 August 2007

45   'Bill Gates, 'United Kingdom launch of Windows Vista and 2007 Microsoft Office System at the British Library, Transcript of remarks by Bill Gates', Microsoft News Centre, 30 January 2007

46   Sumet Jumsai, 'Case Study 4 – Thailand, House on Stilts, Pointer to South East Asian Cultural Origin', in Robert Powell (ed.), *Architecture and*

Identity, Concept Media / The Aga Khan Award for Architecture, Singapore, 1983

47   Peter Raisbeck, 'Marine and Underwater Cities 1960-1975', *Additions to Architectural History*, XIXth Annual Conference of the Society of Architectural Historians, Australia and New Zealand, 2002

48   For more information on designs for floating cities from the 1960s and 70s, see Sandra Kaji-O'Grady and Peter Raisbeck, 'Prototype Cities in the Sea', *The Journal of Architecture*, volume 10, issue 4, 2005, and Raffaele Pernice, *Metabolist Movement between Tokyo Bay Planning and Urban Utopias in the Years of Rapid Economic Growth 1958-1964*, 2007

49   'Noodtoestand in IJsland na uitbarsting vulkaan', *de Volkskrant*, 21 March 2010

50   Lolke van der Heide, 'Luchtvaart raamt vulkaanschade op 1,26 miljard', *NRC Handelsblad*, 21 April 2010

51   Cathelijne Nuijsink, 'Architects should develop generating principles', *Mark – Another Architecture*, issue 27, August / September 2010

52   Jacob Siebelink, 'Bouwen op gebroken aarde', *Reformatorisch Dagblad*, 25 January 2005

53   Tracy Metz, 'Red de wereld, bouw op water', *NRC Handelsblad*, 18 December 2009

Wikipedia, an invaluable source of information, has been consulted many times while writing this book.

Credits

PHOTO CREDITS

Actueel Hoogtebestand Nederland (Current Netherlands Height File): *145*
Ahmad Faizal Yahya / Dreamstime: *195*
Akio Kawasumi / Tange Associates: *273*
Amandah Su Perkins / Dreamstime: *287* (top)
Amsterdam City Archive: *181*
András Győrfi: *237*
Anely Guerrero / Dreamstime: *74* (bottom)
Anne Holtrop / Roderick van der Weijden / Studio Noach: *185* (top)
Anouk Stricher / Dreamstime: *114*
Anthony Ling: *236* (bottom)
Anton Hlushchenko / Dreamstime: *29*
Archigram Archival Project, University of Westminster: *271, 272*
Architecture Research Office and dlandstudio: *132, 133* (bottom)
Arup Biomimetics: *54*
Beeldbank Regional Archive Leiden: *149* (top)
Beeldbank Rijkswaterstaat: *154* (bottom left and bottom right), *155, 156* (top right)
Braendan Yong / Dreamstime: *221* (bottom left)
Burning Man: *36*
C. Mayhew and R. Simmon (NASA/ GSFC): *23* (bottom)
Camilla Maia: *16*
CASA architecten: *90*
Christopher Rawlins / Dreamstime: *189* (top)

City Archives Amsterdam: *63* (top)
Corsmit / Royal Haskoning: *91* (top)
Cosanti Foundation: *270* (top)
Cruquiusmuseum: *150*
Daimler Global Media Site: *284*
Daniël Leppens / Dreamstime: *208*
Danilo Mongiello / Dreamstime: *180*
David Davis / Dreamstime: *120*
Deborah Coles / Dreamstime: *211*
Digitalized by Google: *213*
Dirk Sigmund / Dreamstime: *197* (top)
Doriann Kransberg / Amsterdam City Archive: *277*
Dura Vermeer: *59*
Dutch Docklands: *34-35, 52-53, 62, 89, 98, 101, 174, 182, 187, 188, 190, 192* (bottom), *193, 216-217, 218, 225* (bottom), *292*
Earth Sciences and Image Analysis Laboratory, NASA Johnson Space Center: *118* (left)
Edurivero / Dreamstime: *118* (right)
Ellywa: *83* (right)
Emerson Stepp: *236* (top)
Eric Gevaert / Dreamstime: *142, 149* (bottom)
Estate of R. Buckminster Fuller: *274-275*
Ewa Walicka / Dreamstime: *192* (top)
Femke de Wild: *197* (middle and bottom)
Flaxton: *95*
Frank Palmer: *31* (top)
Freek de Vos: *63* (bottom)
Galyna Andrushko / Dreamstime: *189* (bottom)
Gary Eason / Dreamstime: *172*
Guillaume Paumier: *287* (bottom)

Guy Nordenson and Associates, Catherine Seavitt Studio, and Architecture Research Office with Lizzie Hodges, Marianne Koch, James Smith, and Michael Tantala: *133* (top)
Hannah Anthonysz: *240* (bottom), *241*
Henri Cormont / Beeldbank Rijkswaterstaat: *75* (left and right)
Houstondowntown.com: *85*
Ippirolf / Dreamstime: *224*
Isabel Poulin / Dreamstime: *125* (top)
Itoshin87: *288*
Iwan Baan: *20-21* (top and bottom left)
Jacques Rougerie: *270* (bottom)
Jan Kranendonk / Dreamstime: *285* (top)
Javier Gil / Dreamstime: *290*
JDS: *56-57*
Jillessa Gammon: *176-177*
John H.: *175*
Joop van Houdt / Beeldbank Rijkswaterstaat: *144* (bottom)
Jrockar / Dreamstime: *121* (left)
Klosz007 / Dreamstime: *240* (top)
Koen Olthuis / Waterstudio: *34-35, 46, 48* (bottom left), *51, 52-53, 55, 62, 65, 68, 98, 101* (bottom left and bottom right), *103, 105* (bottom), *106, 134-135, 163, 164-165, 166, 182, 187, 188, 190, 192* (bottom), *193, 216-217, 218, 225* (bottom), *282, 292*
Koninklijke Bibliotheek (National Library of the Netherlands), the Hague: *247*

Float!
Building on Water to Combat Urban
Congestion and Climate Change

Publisher
Frame Publishers

Authors
Koen Olthuis
David Keuning

Production
Sarah Schultz (Frame Publishers)

Graphic design
Adriaan Mellegers (Frame Publishers)

Translation
Christine Gardner (InOtherWords)

Copy editing
D'Laine Camp (InOtherWords)

Image research
Ankie Stam (Waterstudio.NL)
Lucas Wetzels (Waterstudio.NL)
Tim van Bentum (kantoorvanbentum)
Stephen Killion (Frame Publishers)

Prepress
Edward de Nijs (Frame Publishers)

Printing
D'Print, Singapore

Trade distribution USA and Canada
Consortium Book Sales
& Distribution, LLC.
34 Thirteenth Avenue NE, Suite 101
Minneapolis, MN 55413-1007
United States
T +1 612 746 2600
T +1 800 283 3572 (orders)
F +1 612 746 2606

Distribution rest of world
Frame Publishers
Laan der Hesperiden 68
1076 DX Amsterdam
The Netherlands
www.framemag.com
distribution@framemag.com

ISBN: 978-90-77174-29-6

© 2010 Frame Publishers,
Amsterdam, 2010

Whilst every effort has been
made to ensure accuracy, Frame
Publishers does not under any
circumstances accept responsibility
for errors or omissions. Any
mistakes or inaccuracies will be
corrected in case of subsequent
editions upon notification to the
publisher.

The Koninklijke Bibliotheek lists
this publication in the Nederlandse
Bibliografie: detailed bibliographic
information is available on the
internet at http://picarta.pica.nl

Printed on acid-free paper produced
from chlorine-free pulp. TCF ∞
Printed in China

9 8 7 6 5 4 3 2 1